Contents

· WARD LOCK MASTER GARDENER ·

Cottage Gardening

ANNE STEVENS

WARD LOCK

First published in Great Britain in 1994
by Ward Lock, Villiers House, 41/47 Strand,
London WC2N 5JE, England
A Cassell Imprint

British Library Cataloguing in Publication Data
is available upon application from The British Library

ISBN 0 7063 7213 1

Text filmset by Litho Link Ltd, Welshpool, Powys, Wales
Printed and bound in Singapore by Craft Print Pte Ltd

Previous page: **Mass
plantings of herbaceous
perennials and shrubs to
give a cottage garden effect.**

A modern well-filled herbaceous border that captures the true cottage garden style.

Preface

For many people cottage gardening conjures up a picture of pretty little cottages with their thatched roofs and porches over which climbing roses, honeysuckle and clematis have been trained. The typical cottage garden has, many people believe, always been filled with a wonderful profusion of annuals, perennials and bulbs, many grown for their fragrance. Lilies, lavender, roses and sweet peas were the traditionally grown plants for their marvellous scent and still are today.

But this is, in fact, a rather romantic view. The true cottage gardens of yesteryear contained mainly vegetables and fruit used to feed the cottager and his family. Chickens, ducks, pigs and sometimes a cow were kept to provide supplementary eggs, meat and milk.

Nowadays we grow more flowers in our cottage gardens but many of us will still find some spaces to squeeze in some fruit trees or bushes, along with one or two rows of vegetables.

I have always liked cottages and their gardens and am very lucky to live in a thatched cottage with a large garden. Here you will find a great range of perennials, bulbs, trees and shrubs. Also, a large kitchen garden where many varieties of fruit and vegetables grow.

I hope that after reading this book you will be encouraged to try cottage gardening for yourself, whether along traditional or modern lines.

A.S.

ACKNOWLEDGEMENTS

The publishers would like to thank the following for supplying photographs for this book: Garden Picture Library: pp. 9, 12, 28, 29, 44, 45 (left), 60, 65, 69, 77, 93; Clive Nichols: pp. 4, 8, 13, 16, 17, 20, 21, 24, 33 (top), 36, 40, 45 (right), 48, 49, 53, 68, 72, 73, 80, 81, 89, 92; Hugh Palmer: p. 56; Wildlife Matters: pp. 32, 33 (bottom), 41, 64.

The line illustrations were drawn by Vana Haggerty F.L.S., Nils Solberg and David Woodroffe.

· 1 ·
What is Cottage Gardening?

Old cottage gardens, although on first sight a glorious jumble of wonderful flowers, fruit and vegetables, were in fact a clever design of organized informality. Massed flowers spilled out over paths and steps while marvellous vegetables grew with great abundance.

There were orchards and paddocks where sheep or goats were kept, together with a house cow that supplied the cottager with milk and cream. Surplus milk was used to make butter and cheese.

A collection of chickens, ducks and geese were kept to provide the cottager and his family with eggs and meat.

Nearly all cottages had a pig sty where they kept just one or two pigs. Their meat would be used for pork, or smoked or salted for bacon and ham. The pigs were fed on scraps from the kitchen, such as vegetable peelings, so nothing was wasted. Sometimes pigs would be allowed to forage in the orchard, eating the windfall apples. They also helped to root up the weeds.

Some cottagers would keep bees and there were several reasons for doing this. The bees provided the family with honey which was used for sweetening the cakes and drinks. The beeswax was used for making candles and furniture polish. Another good reason for keeping bees was that they helped pollinate all sorts of fruit, and also vegetables like broad and runner beans. There are still many people that keep bees, in towns as well as in the country. Indeed, hives look very

attractive in a garden. However, if you keep bees you must make sure that there are enough plants with nectar-producing flowers to feed the bees. Fruit trees and hawthorn will give a good supply and also many of the wild flowers including primroses, celandines, daisies and clover.

Lawns
Traditional small cottage gardens had little or no areas of lawn, as it was thought to be a waste of space that could be used more productively for vegetables or fruit. More often there were just strips of grass to divide flower borders or to use as a path. If there was a lawn it would often have a small round flower bed in the centre of it, sometimes with a narrow gravel path surrounding the whole area.

COTTAGE GARDENS TODAY

Whether you live in a town or in the country it is relatively easy to create a cottage garden. Cottage gardens should look informal without being very untidy. It is important that the right kinds of plants are used and that they will fit in with their surroundings and any features that are in the garden (Fig. 1, page 10).

Flower borders
Flowers need to be mass planted regardless of whether they are perennials, biennials, annuals

7

or bulbs. Flower borders can be any shape or size depending on how many flowers you want to grow and how much room there is available. Another factor is the type of soil you have in your garden. It is no good trying to grow moisture-loving perennials in a chalky free-draining soil. Try to grow the plants that will do well in your soil.

• *Sun or shade?* Most flowers, and certainly almost all annuals, will grow best in a sunny position but some plants prefer to be in shade. These are mainly perennials and bulbs.

If you have a wide herbaceous border in a sunny position that has a good depth of rich soil, the range of plants you can grow is vast. The selection needs plenty of thought, as certain points should be taken into consideration, but in the end it is all a matter of personal choice. You will have to decide if you want year-round colour,

or perhaps a special colour scheme, and if the perennial plants will be mixed with annuals. All these questions will need to be answered before planting can begin.

Traditional perennial borders

For traditional herbaceous borders that have tall perennials at the back, try including some of the following: delphiniums, lupins, Michaelmas daisies, Japanese anemones, phlox, aruncus and macleaya.

When it comes to medium-sized perennials the list is almost endless and many are true old cottage-garden plants. Use old varieties of aquilegias, hardy geraniums, penstemons, day lilies and eryngiums. In front of these grow violas, arabis, omphalodes, dwarf campanulas and prunella.

Bulbs can be planted in between: daffodils, hyacinths and tulips for spring, followed by alliums, camassia and gladioli for summer flowering. Bulbs are perennial plants as they come up every year.

Annual and biennial borders

You can have borders completely devoted to annuals or mixed with biennials. Front gardens of old cottages were often quite small and annuals were often planted in beds and borders here. Some of the plantings were quite formal, with straight rows of alyssum, lobelia, antirrhinums, bedding salvias and zinnias. Other planting schemes were more informal, with half-hardy annual seed sown in patches. The seed was sown directly in the soil.

◀ A traditional perennial border featuring delphiniums to give both height and colour.

▶ A charming cottage garden with a wonderful border, overflowing with cottage garden plants.

Biennials often bloom in late spring and were mixed with summer-flowering annuals to give a longer flowering season. The seed of biennials were sown in the vegetable garden in the previous spring, then moved to where they were to bloom in the autumn. This is true of most biennials except honesty (*Lunaria annua*) the seed of which you should sow where you want the flowers to grow.

More people should grow biennials today as many are true old cottage-garden plants. Think of the cup-and-saucer canterbury bells, wallflowers, Siberian wallflowers, forget-me-nots and hollyhocks.

Hollyhock (*Alcea rosea*) is really a perennial but not a very long-lasting one and is best grown as a biennial. Sow the seed in early summer and they will bloom the following year. The hollyhock flowers are loved by bees and butterflies. There are both single and double-flowered varieties.

Bulbs and corms for cut flowers

Bulbs and corms were not often grown in borders on their own, they tended to be planted between shrubs and perennials. Occasionally they were planted in small beds in the front garden, in which case hyacinths, tulips and anemones were mainly used.

Anemones *A. coronaria* 'St Brigid' was a favourite with its semi-double flowers and is still widely grown today. It comes in a range of colours including red, pink, white and shades of blue and mauve, and is a very long-lived cut flower.

Anemone corms planted in the autumn will bloom in late spring and early summer.

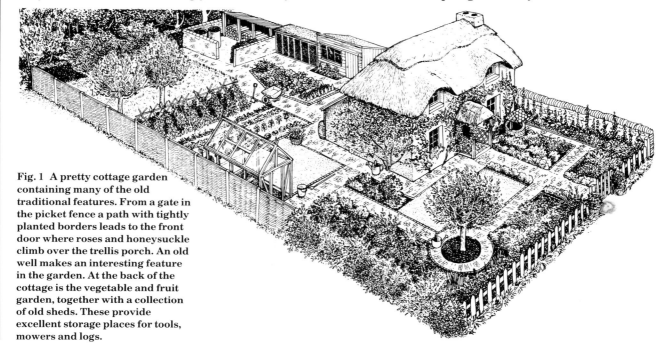

Fig. 1 A pretty cottage garden containing many of the old traditional features. From a gate in the picket fence a path with tightly planted borders leads to the front door where roses and honeysuckle climb over the trellis porch. An old well makes an interesting feature in the garden. At the back of the cottage is the vegetable and fruit garden, together with a collection of old sheds. These provide excellent storage places for tools, mowers and logs.

· HANDY TIP ·

Allow biennials and short-lived perennials to self-seed in the flower borders. That way you will have plenty of young seedlings to take the place of the old plants.

Annuals like love-in-a-mist and candytuft should also be left to self-seed.

Dahlias, although not bulbs or corms as they grow from a tuber, should be included as they were planted either in borders or on their own or mixed with annuals and perennials. Dahlias were grown and still are as a cut flower. They will bloom all summer and into autumn when frost will cut them down. People tend to grow dahlias in rows in the vegetable garden and on allotments, and they are often grown specially for showing at flower shows.

There are so many different kinds of dahlias, from the tiny pompon to medium-sized cactus and decorative ones, then right up to giant-sized dahlias with huge blooms bigger than a large dinner plate. Flowers can be of nearly any colour, some being bi-coloured.

Unless you live in an area where the winters are mild, dahlias should be treated as half-hardy plants. The tubers are planted in late spring when the risk of frost has passed and then dug up in the autumn after the foliage has been caught by the frost. Cut off the stems to within 8 cm (3 in) of the tubers, shake or wash the soil off the tubers and dry in a light airy place. When they are completely dry, store them in a dry frost-free shed or garage. Some people like to store them in wooden boxes, covering the tubers with dry wood shavings or peat. Often this does help to stop them going mouldy and rotten in damp cold weather.

Dahlias like to grow in a sunny position in good soil. They need plenty of water when flowering but will reward you with many months of beautiful cut flowers.

Gladioli were grown in the vegetable garden as a cut flower. The corms were planted in spring for summer flowering, and when the foliage had died down in the autumn the corms were dug up and dried, to be replanted the following year in the spring. The gladioli used for cut flowers are hybrids and should be treated as half-hardy; only in sheltered districts can they be left outside during the winter.

If you do not want the bother of lifting gladioli in the autumn, grow *Gladiolus byzantinus* instead, as it is hardy and the corms can be left in the ground. This gladiolus is best planted in a border between perennials or low-growing shrubs. The purple-red flowers come out in early summer.

PRODUCE IN THE GARDEN

Only fruit and vegetables were grown in the majority of old cottage gardens, as cottagers had to supply their families with home-grown food; there was no going to the greengrocers for such items then. They even grew vegetables in their front gardens.

Vegetables
Vegetables always occupied the most fertile and productive areas of a garden, with pockets of poor soil used for flowers.

Large vegetable plots or borders were rectangular in shape, bordered by grass or gravel paths. These paths were nearly always made wide enough to be able to push a wheelbarrow along them – an important point to remember today when too many of us make working in a small garden unnecessarily difficult for ourselves by building paths which are too narrow.

The rectangular bed system is still being used as this well-tried and tested way of growing vegetables is one of the best. However the beds are likely to be smaller, or long narrow borders created.

Fruit
Fruit was grown in the kitchen garden, in orchards or against a wall. Apples, pears, plums, cherries and medlars were planted in paddocks, orchards and in amongst boundary hedges. If you have an old hedge around your garden perhaps

you have a damson, sloe or crab apple growing in it. These old trees still produce quite good crops of full-flavoured fruit.

Hazel and cob nuts also grew in hedges, as well as in thickets in a corner of a field or wood. Hazels were very important in country life, providing materials for pea sticks, bean poles, spars for thatching and wood for making hurdles.

Soft fruits were planted in vegetable plots and trained against the cottage walls. The walls gave protection for fruit like apricots, peaches and figs, as well as loganberries and vines.

WILDLIFE AND WILD FLOWERS

Old cottage gardens contained all kinds of wildlife, some good for the garden and others, like rabbits and mice, very destructive. Some wild flowers were encouraged to grow in the garden, mingling with the cultivated plants.

Today when everyone should try to use less chemicals in the garden, it is important that we should make our gardens inviting to some wildlife. By having the right habitat and suitable plants, they will hopefully help to keep the garden free from pests.

Birds
Birds are very essential but they will need shrubs and trees for cover and nesting sites; in return they will eat slugs, snails, aphids and caterpillars. Thrushes and blackbirds will eat many pests but in the autumn and winter they supplement their diet with berries and fruit. Hollies, cotoneasters, sorbus and hawthorns are trees and

◄ **Vegetables were grown in great abundance in old cottage gardens, and still are today as this picture shows.**

► **Attract bees and butterflies to your garden by planting late summer-flowering sedums.**

shrubs that will provide berries for the birds to eat. Starlings will eat leather-jackets so should be enticed into a garden. We must not forget robins, always associated with cottage gardens, as they eat many harmful insects. You will often see a robin hopping about while you are gardening; it's hoping that a tasty morsel will get turned up during any digging or weeding.

Remember to put out water in shallow bowls for the birds to drink, in dry and also frosty weather. Keep windfall apples in a box to feed them in very cold weather.

Frogs, toads and slow-worms

Old cottage gardens were likely places to have a damp ditch along a boundary, or there may have been a pond in a nearby farmyard, but they did not have small man-made ponds and pools like we have now. We are lucky that today pools are easily constructed or come ready-made, because as more of them are incorporated in our gardens, frogs and toads have also been increasing in numbers. They will eat many slugs, snails and woodlice and are generally very useful to have around. Slow-worms, which are legless lizards, eat the same type of food, and are also harmless to people.

Bees and butterflies

Bees, butterflies and hoverflies should be encouraged to visit your garden to pollinate flowers, fruit and vegetables. Grow special flowering plants to attract these insects, such as sedums, Michaelmas daisies, buddleias and crocuses.

It is important to have hoverflies in the garden as they will eat aphids. Learn to recognize the different kinds of hoverflies as the large ones look like wasps and are often killed, which is a pity. Wasps themselves will eat blackflies.

Wild flowers

It is nice to include wild flowers in a cottage garden: primroses, bluebells, campions and cow parsley all look lovely mixed with cultivated plants. You can buy wild flower seed, but do not dig up plants from hedgerows or fields.

· BEE AND BUTTERFLY PLANTS ·

Name	Description
Buddleia davidii 'Royal Red'	Tall shrub loved by butterflies; red flowers
Buddleia × weyeriana 'Golden Glow'	Tall shrub with apricot-yellow flowers
Giant scabious (Cephalaria gigantea)	Tall perennial scabious with pale yellow blooms
Hemp agrimony (Eupatorium cannabinum)	Excellent perennial for butterflies; tall stems and pink flowers
Joe pye weed (Eupatorium maculatum atropurpureum)	Tall perennial with dark stems, mauvish-red flowers
Ligularia dentata	Tall perennial with large yellow daisy flowers
Michaelmas daisy (Aster)	
• 'Alma Potschke'	Tall perennial with bright pink flowers
• 'Harrington's Pink'	Tall perennial with pink flowers
Mullein (Verbascum thapsus)	Tall spikes of small yellow flowers; grey felty leaves
Oriental poppy (Papaver orientale 'Picotée')	Large orange-red flowers with white centre
Stonecrop (Sedum 'Autumn Cloud')	Late-flowering perennial with deep red tiny flowers
Stonecrop (Sedum 'Sunset Cloud')	Perennial with purple grey leaves; dark red flowers
Tree heather (Erica arborea)	Tall winter-flowering shrub for bees; white flowers
Winter-flowering heather (Erica carnea)	
• 'Myretoun Ruby'	Deep red flowers during winter and spring
• 'Springwood White'	Prostrate-growing heather with white flowers in winter and spring

· 2 ·
Making Beds and Borders

Flower beds and borders of all shapes and sizes were put in any available space not occupied by vegetables and fruit in old cottage gardens. Small beds and narrow borders were squeezed into odd corners, often where ground was not suitable for growing vegetables.

Traditionally there would be colourful borders either side of the path leading to the front door. The informally planted massed flowers would often tumble over the pathway in organized informality. It is this kind of effect that people today want to create, and it is not difficult provided you follow a simple planting plan.

Preparing the border for planting

Perhaps you have just taken over a rather neglected garden with overgrown borders which you would like to dig up and replant. Or maybe you want to reorganize your plants in an established herbaceous border. In either case the best time to tackle this task is early autumn and aim to get the job finished before the weather becomes too wet or cold during the winter.

First of all decide if there are any of the old plants that are worth saving; it is easy to split up perennials and just replant small clumps. However, if there are old untidy straggly shrubs, it is often difficult to prune them back into a good shape, especially as some types cannot be pruned back too hard or they will die. In these cases, it is better to dig them up completely and start again with new plants.

Dig up all the plants you want to keep and put them to one side for replanting. Remove and dispose of all the other plants. Now dig the ground over, removing the roots of any perennial weeds.

Removing perennial weeds

In order to obtain trouble-free borders, it is essential that every piece of root belonging to perennial weeds must be removed. If a single piece of root is left behind of weeds such as ground-elder, convolvulus and couch grass, it will very soon start to grow again. If you have stony soil or clay, you will find it easier to fork out the roots rather than dig with a spade. Never be in a hurry to start replanting unless the ground is completely weed free first.

If the soil has not been dug or used for many years, you will need to feed it. Dig well-rotted manure into the ground if you are able to get it, otherwise bone-meal or spent mushroom compost, which are just as effective.

If you have clay soil or the ground is water-logged, mix gravel, old straw or wood chippings into the soil to lighten it.

After all this work has been done you will be ready to start planting up your border. If weather conditions allow, the planting is best carried out in autumn.

◀ A well-planned herbaceous border with closely planted perennials.

▶ A mixed border where old-fashioned perennials grow in the shade of an old tree.

Type of border

You will now have to decide what type of border will suit your garden and your taste in plants. Borders can be for perennials, annuals, shrubs alone, or a mixed border containing all types of plants.

HERBACEOUS BORDERS

Nothing evokes the cottage-garden look better than traditional herbaceous borders filled to overflowing with perennials for nearly all-the-year-round colour. Colour and interest come from attractive and interesting foliage as well as the flowers and seedheads. The borders do not have to be large, but you do have to be more selective with your choice of plants in small borders as you do not want vigorous growers swamping dainty plants.

Making a plan

Some people like to draw out a plan of where the plants are to go, working out the best positions for certain plants, with the tall ones at the back of the border. Other people prefer just to stand the plants on top of the soil where they are to be planted. These can be moved about until they are exactly in the right position.

Remember that some plants are very vigorous and need to be spaced 60 cm (24 in) apart. These include phlox and the old cottage-garden favourite shasta daisy (*Leucanthemum max-*

imum). Others, like rock roses and thrift (*Armeria maritima*), need only to be 30 cm (12 in) apart.

Never put in plants with dry roots. Water the plants in pots and soak bare-rooted plants in a bucket of water before they are planted.

Planting

Do not plant if the soil is very wet or if it is frozen. Wait until you have the right conditions, and in the meantime give bare-rooted perennials some protection against frost damage should the weather be very cold.

If you are replanting perennials dug up from weed-infested borders, make sure that there are no pieces of weed roots mixed with the roots of the perennial. Otherwise you risk re-introducing weeds to a clean border. It does not hurt the perennial to tease out their roots thoroughly, removing every piece of weed. Although this is rather fiddly, it will save time in the long run.

When planting, dig out a good-size hole, spread out the roots of the perennials, fill in and firm the soil down round the plant. Do not plant too deeply: the soil should be level with the crown of the plant.

When you have finished planting, you should give each plant a good watering. (See Chapter 10 for aftercare and maintenance.)

MIXED SHRUB AND PERENNIAL BORDERS

If you want to have a mixed shrub and perennial border it will require more space than one for perennials or annuals alone. The border will need to be at least 1.8 m (6 ft) wide, otherwise you will need to prune the shrubs endlessly to stop them from swamping the perennials.

The shrubs should be at the back of the border with the perennials in front. Bulbs and small groups of annuals can be planted between the

perennials to give a longer season of colour. Shrubs need to be planted 1.2–1.8 m (4–6 ft) apart, depending on how vigorous they are.

Shrubs were not so widely grown in old cottage gardens as they took up so much space, and for most people fruit and vegetables needed to be given priority. However, shrubs are more popular in the modern cottage garden, with new varieties appearing all the time. They are reasonably labour-saving: just prune them once a year to keep them in shape.

Shrubs for mixed borders

Before making a final selection of your choice of shrubs for your border, consider the following factors: do you want evergreen shrubs, shrubs

Fig. 2 Planting bare-rooted and container-grown perennials.

(a) When planting a bare-rooted hosta, spread out the roots before putting the plant in the hole.

(b) Fill in hole and firm the plant in well.

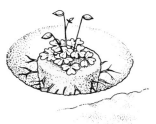

(c) When planting a container-grown perennial, tease out roots that have become tangled before putting the plant in the ground (d).

for autumn colour or shrubs that are grown for their flowers? The list of possibilities is enormous.

Think how much space you have available and how big the shrubs will eventually grow. They will be small when first planted and a common fault is to plant them too close together. If you do not like to see large expanses of bare soil in between, plant ground-cover perennials or hardy annuals to fill the gaps while the shrubs mature.

● *Large shrubs* The large, taller shrubs will provide both a windbreak and a background for the shorter shrubs and perennials growing in front of them.

Buddleias Always find room for one or two buddleias in your mixed border, not only for the flowers but to encourage bees and butterflies to come into your garden. Buddleias are the best shrubs for this purpose. There are many species and varieties which will give flowers all summer and well into autumn in addition.

The first to bloom is the orange-ball tree (*Buddleia globosa*) in early summer. It has fragrant orangy-yellow ball-shaped heads of tiny flowers that are favoured by Small Tortoiseshell butterflies.

During the summer the butterfly bush (*Buddleia davidii*) will be in flower, attracting many kinds of butterflies including Red Admirals, Painted Ladies and Peacocks, as well as other sorts of insects like bees and moths. *Buddleia davidii* 'Black Knight' has very dark purple flowers and is excellent for the back of a border; if this does not tone in with your colour scheme, plant the lovely white-flowered *B. davidii* 'White Cloud', which grows quite vigorously but suits any type of soil that is not too wet.

Rubus *R.* 'Benenden' is a tall shrub that prefers free-draining soil in a sunny position. It has gracefully arching branches that can be 2.1 m (7 ft) in length. In early summer large white single blooms are produced all along the branches. Immediately after flowering, the shrub needs to be pruned, by just cutting out the old flowering branches. New ones will soon grow during the summer and they will produce flowers the next year.

Tamarisk (*Tamarix tetrandra*) is a tall graceful-looking shrub with long racemes of tiny pink flowers that appear in early summer. It has narrow leaves and dark stems that show up well against the pink feathery flower spikes. It likes a sunny site in well-drained soil, but will tolerate other conditions as well. Excellent for growing in very windy positions and also as a hedge in coastal areas.

Weigela *W.* 'Bristol Ruby' is a fairly medium to tall, vigorous-growing shrub which is also very useful for the back of the border. It has bright red flowers in early summer, produced all along the long, slightly curving stems. It is another shrub that needs to be pruned hard after flowering, otherwise it will get very leggy and untidy. It will grow in almost any type of soil in sun or slight shade.

● *Medium shrubs* Some shrubs are grown more for their foliage rather than their flowers.

Philadelphus *P. coronarius* 'Aureus' has bright yellow leaves in spring which turn greeny yellow in summer. It has white fragrant flowers in summer but they do not show up well against the golden foliage. By pruning out some of the old wood each year it can be kept at a height of about 1.2 m (4 ft). It has good contrasting foliage when planted next to the purple-leafed **Berberis thunbergii atropurpurea**, new leaves of which are almost red at first. This shrub has pale yellow flowers in spring followed by red berries.

One or two evergreens should be included in a mixed border to give colour during the winter months, and if you plant skimmias you will have good winter foliage plus bright berries. **Skimmias** are compact-growing shrubs which

· SHRUBS FOR MIXED BORDERS ·	
Name	**Description**
Beauty bush (*Kolkwitzia amabilis*)	Pretty pink flowers in early summer
Cherry laurel (*Prunus laurocerasus* 'Castlewellan')	Evergreen shrub with green and white variegated leaves
Chinese bush cherry (*Prunus glandulosa* 'Alba plena')	Dwarf double white-flowered cherry
Cotton lavender (*Santolina chamaecyparissus*)	Silvery, finely cut foliage, yellow flowers
Daisy bush (*Olearia stellulata*)	Evergreen shrub with white daisy flowers in late spring
Flowering nutmeg (*Leycesteria formosa*)	Grown for its maroon berries
Golden elder (*Sambucus racemosa*)	Cut-leaved golden elder
Hedgehog holly (*Ilex aquifolium* 'Ferox Argentea')	Very prickly, variegated holly; slow growing
Indian currant (*Symphoricarpos* 'Foliis Variegatis')	Small shrub with tiny yellow-green leaves
Lilac (*Syringa × josiflexa* 'Bellicent')	Dark pink flowers in bud, opening to pale pink
Mock orange (*Philadelphus* 'Beauclerk')	Large fragrant white blooms in summer
Oregon grape (*Mahonia aquifolium*)	Glossy green foliage with clusters of tiny yellow flowers
Snowball bush (*Viburnum opulus* 'Roseum')	White sterile flowers that look like snowballs.
Spanish gorse (*Genista hispanica*)	Compact bush covered with yellow flowers in summer
Witch hazel (*Hamamelis mollis*)	Unusual yellow flowers in winter

◄ A mixed border featuring spiraea, in front of which are planted tulips and daffodils.

► A good mixed border can contain roses, shrubs and perennials.

will eventually reach the height of 90 cm (3 ft) and hardly ever need any pruning. They prefer to grow in slightly acid soil, otherwise the leaves will often turn yellow. They will grow in sun or light shade.

Skimmia japonica has glossy dark green, elongated leaves with clusters of tiny white flowers in early spring, producing bright red waxy berries in late summer which will stay until early spring unless eaten by birds during the winter. It is a female plant and in order to get a good pollination to set the berries you will need to plant *Skimmia japonica* 'Rubella' nearby. The latter is a male plant which has large clusters of creamy white flowers in early spring. Both skimmias are wonderful for winter colour and scent.

Skimmia laureola should be grown more often than it is nowadays. It has glossy green leaves and large heads of fragrant, tiny, greenish-yellow

flowers in spring. A small compact shrub only 75 cm (2½ ft) tall, it will tolerate most kinds of soil but not wet ones.

Spiraeas are very free-flowering, medium-sized shrubs for sunny positions in most types of soil. *Spiraea japonica* 'Anthony Waterei' will flower for many weeks during summer, producing clusters of small bright pinky red flowers. Sometimes in spring the new foliage will be pink and cream variegated, which will eventually turn green during the summer.

If you like bright foliage, grow *S. japonica* 'Goldflame', which has brilliant yellow and orangy-red leaves in spring and early summer, with deep pink flowers. Prune quite hard in early spring to encourage the shrub to produce many new shoots with the bright foliage.

Another shrub which has outstanding foliage is **Weigela 'Florida Variegata'** which has cream-edged variegated green leaves and has lovely pale pink flowers in summer. A medium-growing shrub, not as vigorous as other weigelas.

Perennials

Once the shrubs have been planted some perennials can then be put in front of them (Fig. 2). Next to the shrubs plant tall perennials like lupins, phlox, penstemons and oriental poppies. In front of these put in some clumps of the shorter varieties of hardy geraniums, together with pinks and pansies to give an informal look to the border.

Bulbs can be planted between the shrubs and perennials to create extra colour in the border. Daffodils, crocuses and snowdrops are all suitable for this purpose.

FRAGRANT MIXED BORDERS

Lovely fragrant mixed borders conjure up a romantic garden picture of trellis-backed roses, lilies, pinks, carnations and violets.

Start the planting with the shrubs as described in the discussion on mixed borders, which can be found on pages 17–20.

Fragrant shrubs

Lavender is a must for every fragrant border, and the variety *Lavandula angustifolia* 'Hidcote' has deep violet flowers and is a compact bush. All lavenders like well-drained soil and a sunny position. Trim after flowering to keep the bush in a good shape.

Fig. 3 A trellis or a rope strung between stout supports makes an excellent background for fragrant borders.

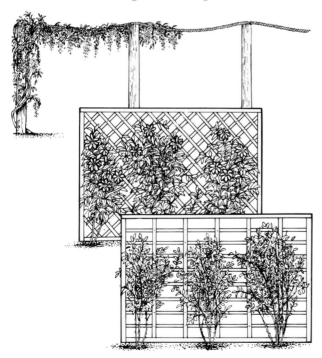

Plant some shrubs that flower during the winter months. The shrubby **honeysuckle** (*Lonicera fragrantissima*) has lovely cream flowers during late winter and spring before the leaves appear. The flowers also have a wonderful scent and a few stems picked and taken indoors will fill a cottage or house with fragrance. A tall, fairly vigorous shrub for the back of a border.

It's worth while having at least one or two evergreen shrubs in the border, and one of the best fragrant evergreens is **Osmanthus delavayi**, which is covered with small, very sweetly scented white flowers in late spring and has small glossy, dark green leaves. It is best near the back of the border as it will grow to over 1.8 m (6 ft) if it is allowed to. Prune back after flowering if you do not want such a tall shrub.

Lilacs give delightful scent but some like the common lilac (*Syringa vulgaris*) are quite large. This shrub is sometimes too vigorous in growth and needs plenty of space; it also has the annoying habit of suckering. *Syringa microphylla* 'Superba' is a more suitable shrub for mixed borders as it only grows 90 cm (3 ft) tall. It has clusters of tiny pink fragrant flowers during summer, and will grow in most soils, including chalky ones.

Roses

No cottage garden is complete without a few roses, and there are so many different types of roses that will fit in with any garden design.

Many people favour hybrid tea roses but shrub roses are more suitable for a cottage garden and are usually more fragrant. With so many varieties and species to choose from it is difficult to pick out just one or two, although one of my favourites is the hybrid musk rose called 'Buff Beauty', which has lovely apricot yellow blooms and will repeat flowering.

Fragrant perennials for borders

In front of the shrubs the area should be filled with a wide selection of fragrant perennials. Try to include scented peonies, pinks, carnations, sweet rocket and perennial honesty.

Sweet rocket or dame's violet (*Hesperis matronalis*) is a true old cottage-garden perennial, producing tall 90 cm (3 ft) branching stems that are covered with small, very fragrant white or pale mauve flowers in spring or early summer. Not a very long-lived perennial but it self-seeds freely.

Perennial **honesty** (*Lunaria rediviva*) looks very much like hesperis. Its tall stems grow up from rosettes of attractive, serrated, heart-shaped leaves. The scented flowers are pale lilac, blooming in late spring, and are followed by lovely silvery white seed-pods.

Fragrant annuals such as stocks, godetia and sweet peas can be grown between the perennials.

FRAGRANT HERB BED

The cartwheel herb bed is one of the most popular designs and is attractive to look at (Fig. 4). Bricks or small slabs are laid down to form a path round the bed. The bed itself is divided into sections in which a different type of herb is planted. You can have as many sections as you wish but six or eight are usual. The sections are divided by bricks laid on the surface, or by slabs set into the ground. Slabs are better as they will help to contain vigorous-growing herbs like mint.

The sections could contain mint, chives, parsley, sage, thyme and fennel. On the centre of the wheel stands a container in which may be grown the half-hardy shrub lemon verbena (now known as *Aloysia triphylla*, but formerly *Lippia citriodora*). The leaves, when touched or crushed, will fill the air with a wonderful lemon scent.

Fig. 4 A cartwheel herb bed with a planted tub as a centre feature.

·3·

Cottage Garden Perennials

Massed perennials in beds and borders are a traditional feature of any cottage garden, whether it is large or small. They will give you months of colour from flowers, attractive or variegated foliage and even seed-heads.

It is most important that there is colour throughout the year and not just in the summer. Even on a cold, gloomy day in winter you should be able to look from a window and see flowers blooming outside. Nowadays there is such a vast range of reliable, easy-to-grow perennials to choose from for every type of soil and situation, you can take your pick from old well-known varieties and also many new ones.

If perennials are correctly planted they can help to produce a labour-saving garden (Fig. 5). Planting distances between perennials will vary according to the size and vigour of a plant. For example pinks and primroses should be about 30 cm (12 in) apart, while lupins and delphiniums should be spaced about 60 cm (24 in) apart. If planted at these distances, they will soon grow to cover any bare soil in between and help to smother any annual weeds that start to come up. Also, by growing perennials fairly close together you may not need to stake tall plants so much as they will help to keep one another up. Using too many stakes does spoil the look of any border.

◄ **Lupins made an excellent background for the shorter-growing plants in this herbaceous border.**

SPRING-FLOWERING PERENNIALS

After a cold, wet winter it is a welcome sight to see the spring-flowering perennials come into bloom. Primroses, polyanthus, pulmonarias and hellebores are great favourites, as they create colourful displays especially when interplanted with spring-flowering bulbs such as snowdrops, crocuses and daffodils.

Hellebores
The lovely lenten rose (*Helleborus orientalis*) blooms throughout the spring months. It likes to grow in good soil, in half or full shade and will sometimes bloom earlier than expected, during the winter, unless there has been frosty weather, in which case buds may be damaged. It is a good idea to remove most of the old leaves in late winter as they often look scorched and untidy; also without so many leaves, the flowers show up so much more. Today there are many different colour forms available, ranging from green, white, spotted to dark maroon.

Primroses and polyanthus
Primroses have always been grown in cottage gardens where their lovely pale yellow flowers herald the arrival of spring. Although they will grow in the sun, they prefer a half-shady position under shrubs, trees or along the base of a hedge, which is closer to their natural habitat. Primroses like soil that does not dry out too much in summer

Fig. 5 Planting distances between perennials will vary depending on the ultimate size of the plant.

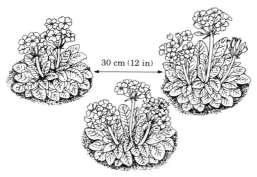

(a) Small perennials like pinks and primulas should be 30 cm (12 in) apart.

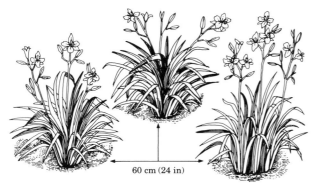

(b) Medium-sized perennials like hardy geraniums, hemerocallis and phlox should be 60 cm (24 in) apart.

and, given the right conditions, will seed freely. There are now many varieties of coloured primroses available which include ones with blue, red, pink or white blooms. If you like to keep to a particular colour scheme in your garden these primroses are ideal as there are so many colours to choose from.

Even more lovely are the double primroses. There are many varieties available, both old and new, all worth searching for. Try the following

varieties of double primroses: *Primula vulgaris* 'Alba Plena' with beautiful pure white double flowers; *P.* 'Red Paddy' with semi-double red flowers with a white edge; *P.* 'Rhapsody', a more dainty plant with double mauve flowers; and *P.* 'Torchlight' which has beautiful pale yellow, very double flowers.

Polyanthus were widely grown in old cottage gardens where they were often planted in a row along the edge of the vegetable plot to provide plenty of cut flowers for the spring. They come in an amazing range of colours, including the large-flowered bright blue *Primula* 'Pacific Giants' and *P.* 'Crescendo' (mixed colours) which come in shades of pink, yellow, orange, red and white, and are also large flowered. Polyanthus prefer to grow in rich soil that does not dry out completely during the summer. They are useful for spring bedding displays interplanted with either daffodils or tulips.

A more dainty plant is the charming 'Gold Laced' polyanthus, which produces heads of small dark red flowers that are edged with gold and sometimes silver. They prefer to grow in damp soil in part shade, and every two or three years they need to be lifted and then divided, otherwise the plants die away in the centre. Similar in habit and growth is the variety 'Lady Greer', a delightful polyanthus with pale yellow, tinged-pink flowers.

● *Growing primroses and polyanthus from seed*
Both primroses and polyanthus grow easily from seed that should be sown in late winter or early spring. The seeds need to be kept cool in order to germinate well at a temperature of no more than 15°C (60°F). The fine seed should be sown on the top of pots filled with a soilless compost; do not cover the seed. Place the pots in a shady position and do not let the compost dry out. Prick out into

boxes or small pots and keep in a cool shady place. Plant out in the autumn and they will produce flowers in the following spring.

Pulmonarias

Pulmonarias are excellent spring-flowering perennials, sometimes first flowering in the winter months if it is mild and often blooming for many weeks. They are easy to grow and will tolerate most types of soil provided it is not too moist. They are happy in a shady dry position.

Lungwort (*Pulmonaria saccharata*) has blue flowers that are pink when first opening and attractive white-spotted dark green leaves. Another with good foliage is *P. longifolia* 'Bertram Anderson', which has long narrow leaves with white spots and pink flowers that turn to blue after a few days. *P. albocorollata* 'Redstart', with bright pink flowers and light green leaves, is good in dry shade and as a ground-cover plant; although it flowers at its best in spring, it often blooms in autumn and winter as well if the weather is not too frosty.

Pulmonarias are evergreen perennials, but any leaves that die in the summer should be removed, as new leaves will soon grow in their place. They are easy to propagate by division in the autumn or early spring.

SUMMER-FLOWERING PERENNIALS

Beds and borders closely planted with summer-flowering perennials will give glorious displays of colour and foliage throughout the summer months. One tends to think of the traditional cottage border full to overflowing with lupins, delphiniums, phlox, penstemons, aquilegias, pinks and pansies, but there are so many easy and reliable perennials to grow for every type of soil and situation.

· SUMMER-FLOWERING PERENNIALS ·

Name	Description
Bleeding heart *(Dicentra spectablis)*	Heart-shaped red flowers hanging from arching stems
Catmint *(Nepeta faassenii)*	Grey-green leaves with spikes of small lavender flowers
Columbine *(Aquilegia vulgaris)*	Spurs in various colours
Crane's bill *(Geranium pratense)*	Attractive foliage with bright lilac-blue flowers
Day lily *(Hemerocallis* 'Tejas')	Weed-suppressing foliage; reddish bronze flowers
Goat's beard *(Aruncus dioicus)*	Tall, good foliage; plumes of white fluffy flowers
Masterwort *(Astrantia major)*	Flowers like small pincushions in white, pink or greenish colours
Meadow rue *(Thalictrum aquilegifolium)*	Fluffy heads of tiny pink flowers: aquilegia-type leaves
Oriental poppy *(Papaver orientalis* 'Mrs Perry')	Long floppy leaves; large bright pink flowers
Pasque flower *(Pulsatilla vulgaris)*	Mauve blooms followed by attractive seed heads
Pearl everlasting *(Anaphalis margaritacea)*	Green-grey narrow leaves with white everlasting flowers
Purple loosestrife *(Lythrum salicaria)*	Tall spikes of small mauve flowers; narrow leaves
Pyrethrum *(Tanacetum* 'Brenda')	Lovely bright pink single flowers; feathery foliage
Spider wort *(Tradescantia virginiana)*	Dark green foliage; flowers three petalled; blue, white or purple
Sneezeweed *(Helenium* 'Wyndley')	Flowers red with brown centre, fading with age

Aquilegias

Aquilegias are a must for every cottage garden and come in many shapes and colours from the old varieties of columbine or granny's bonnet (*Aquilegia vulgaris*) to the newer long-spurred varieties. They bloom in early summer and will thrive in most types of soil as long as it is not waterlogged, either in a sunny position or slight shade. They are very easy to grow from seed and established plants will self-seed readily.

Astrantias

Astrantias are very adaptable plants, suitable for almost any types of soil, apart from very wet ones. There is a place for them in any size of garden and they will be happy to grow in either sun or half shade.

Masterwort (*Astrantia major*) is a well-loved cottage garden perennial that produces branched stems of pretty pincushion-type flowers in colours that range from white, pink and greeny-white; its leaves are dark green and it grows to a height

of 60 cm (24 in). This perennial is good for drying for winter flower arrangements. Pick the flowers when they are full out and hang them upside down in small bunches to dry.

There are several named varieties available, including *A. major* 'Shaggy' which has large white flowers with green tips; *A. major rubra*, which has dark red flowers and is not so vigorous in growth as the other astrantias; and *A. major* 'Sunningdale Variegated', which is grown mainly for its striking light green and creamy white variegated foliage and is best planted in a sunny position.

Astrantia maxima is a beautiful plant which has bright pink flowers that look like miniature posies, does not make thick clumps like other astrantias and will spread slowly by running roots. It also needs fairly rich soil and associates well with hardy geraniums and penstemons.

Day lilies

The day lily (*Hemerocallis* species) will grow in any type of soil and is a very reliable perennial that will flower well every year. Some varieties are quite vigorous in growth and they will need to be divided about every four years; it is best to do this in the autumn.

The older varieties of day lily tend to have flowers of either yellow, orange or red, but now there are many softer shades and colours available, *Hemerocallis* 'Joan Senior' has nearly white flowers with a greenish throat; *H.* 'Luxury Lace' has lovely pale orange blooms with a slightly mauve tinge; and for a more unusual colour and less vigorous growth, try growing *H.* 'Chicago Royal Robe' which has plum-purple blooms.

Hardy geraniums

Hardy geraniums are another essential plant and are very versatile, coming in many colours and different heights. They will grow in sun or shade and are not fussy about soil conditions as long as it is not too wet.

Varieties of geranium (crane's bill) suitable for the edge of a border or raised bed include *Geranium dalmaticum*, which is a compact plant growing only 15 cm (6 in) tall, bearing pink flowers in late spring, sometimes blooming again in late summer, and with small serrated edged leaves that often turn red with age. *G. cinereum* 'Lawrence Flatman' is a prostrate-growing plant which bears pink flowers with mauve-red veining

on the petals throughout the summer months and likes a sunny position.

For the centre of the border try *Geranium renardii;* it has good foliage with the leaves being slightly grey-green and felty on the underside, and white flowers with a dark veining. *Geranium macrorrhizum* has bright pink flowers and aromatic foliage that will sometimes turn red in the autumn and is a very hardy perennial, good as ground cover in semi-shade.

Of the taller varieties *Geranium psilostemon* is an outstanding plant, exhibiting magenta flowers

► *Astrantia major* bears a profusion of greenish white flower heads in summer. Here it is growing in association with a penstemon.

◄ *Aquilegia vulgaris* is a true cottage garden plant which will grow in sun or slight shade.

with a dark centre during summer, attractive foliage, and height 90 cm (36 in). Slightly more unusual is *Geranium pratense* 'Plenum Violaceum' that has double violet flowers on tall branching stems and grows to 90 cm (36 in).

Geraniums are very easy to propagate by division in the autumn or spring and many varieties can be grown from seed sown in spring or early summer.

· PERENNIALS FOR DRY AND SUNNY SITES ·

Name	Description
Catchfly (*Lychnis viscaria*)	Deep pink head of flowers; sticky buds
Evening primrose (*Oenothera missouriensis*)	Large bright yellow flowers; prostrate growing
Globe thistle (*Echinops ritro*)	Round thistle-like blue flowers on tall stems
Lady's mantle (*Alchemilla mollis*)	Fluffy heads of tiny yellow flowers; good foliage
Kansas gay feather (*Liatris spicata*)	Mauvy pink feathery flowers; spiky leaves
Mullein (*Verbascum nigrum*)	Tall spikes of yellow flowers; large leaves
Red scabious (*Knautia macedonica*)	Red flowers like pin- cushions; free flowering
Rock rose (*Helianthemum* 'Ben Nevis')	Orange flowers with brown centre; prostrate growing
Scabious (*Scabiosa* 'Butterfly Blue')	Mauvy-blue flowers; fingered leaves
Skullcap (*Scutellaria altissima*)	Spikes of mauve and white good seed heads
Star of the Veldt (*Osteospermum ecklonii*)	Large lilac daisies with dark blue centre
Stonecrop (*Sedum spectabile*)	Flat heads of tiny pink flowers, blue-green foliage
Thrift (*Armeria alliacea*)	Bright pink heads of tiny flower, like drumsticks
Toadflax (*Linaria purpurea*)	Tall thin spikes of tiny purple flowers
Valerian (*Centranthus ruber*)	Large heads of small red flowers; fleshy foliage

---

Penstemons

Penstemons are very free-flowering perennials blooming for many months during the summer provided they are dead-headed regularly. Some varieties are only half hardy, but there are many which are fully hardy providing they are grown in free-draining soil (wet winters will often kill them). Penstemons are not very long-lived and it is advisable to renew plants about every three or four years, otherwise the old plants tend to get rather woody and do not produce many flowering stems. They are easy to propagate from cuttings, which should be taken from the plants in spring or summer.

The most hardy varieties include *Penstemon* 'Garnet' with rich red flowers, *P.* 'Hidcote Pink' that has soft mauve flowers, *P. glaber* with pinky mauve flowers and *P. venustus* which has pinky mauve flowers. All these penstemons like to grow in a sunny position.

Poppies

Poppies always create bold splashes of colour in a garden, especially the oriental poppy (*Papaver orientalis*) which blooms in early summer. They are worth growing in a border even though they can be rather floppy and untidy. To help avoid this problem, cut down the plants to ground level immediately after flowering. In addition, try planting them next to late-flowering perennials like Michaelmas daisies and Japanese anemones which will then fill the gap left by cutting down the poppy.

There are so many old and new varieties of poppies to choose from, many brightly coloured but some in paler shades. They like to grow in a sunny position in fairly well-drained soil. If you like soft colours choose between *Papaver* 'Mrs Perry', a lovely salmon pink colour with black

· HANDY TIP ·

If you cut down to ground level perennials such as delphiniums and lupins as soon as they have finished flowering, they will often produce more stems of flowers in late summer and early autumn. It helps to keep the plants well watered in hot dry weather.

blotches, *P.* 'Turkish Delight' with pale pink flowers but no blotches, and *P.* 'Cedric Morris', which has off-white flowers shading to pink with a large black centre – very striking to look at. If you prefer strong hot colours, grow the following varieties: *P.* 'Goliath' with large deep red flowers on tall 1 m (3¼ ft) stems; *P.* 'Picotée', a very showy plant featuring orange-red flowers with a white centre; and the less vigorous *P.* 'Curlilocks' that has bright red flowers with fringed edges to the petals and a dark centre.

EARLY AUTUMN-FLOWERING PERENNIALS

In early autumn there are many interesting and unusual perennials that will be in bloom and these should be more widely grown as autumn colour in herbaceous borders is very important. Many varieties of perennial salvias bloom in the late summer, continuing into autumn until cut down by frosts. Other perennials to grow for early autumn flowering include Japanese anemones, *Physostegia virginiana* and the later-blooming varieties of crocus.

Anemones

The Japanese anemone (*Anemone hybrida*) is a lovely old cottage-garden perennial, enhancing any herbaceous border for many weeks while it blooms, although in some soils it can become rather invasive. *Anemone × hybrida* 'Köunigin Charlotte', which used to be called 'Queen Charlotte', has large pink flowers, height 1.3 m (4½ ft); *A.* 'Bressingham Glow' has semi-double deep pink flowers and grows to 1.06 m (3½ ft); and the lovely *A.* 'Honorine Jobert' has large white flowers.

Physostegias

How attractive the spikes of the obedient plant, *Physostegia virginiana* 'Vivid', look when it is in bloom in early autumn. This variety has mauvy-pink flowers on stiff 75 cm (30 in) stems that never need staking. More unusual is *P. virginiana* 'Variegata' which has spikes of pink flowers on 1.06 m (3½ ft) stems, plus the added attraction of cream and green variegated leaves, and will grow in light shade. There is also a white-flowered variety, *P. virginiana* 'Summer Snow' which has flowers in late summer and early autumn.

Physostegias prefer a rich slightly moist soil and spread fairly quickly by white fleshy roots.

Salvias

Of the many interesting hardy perennial salvias, the following include some of the hardiest provided they are grown in free-draining soil in a sunny position. The plants need to be cut down to ground level in the winter and added protection can be given by mulching the plant thickly with pulverized forest bark, spent mushroom compost or moss peat. Do not be surprised to find that some of the salvias do not start to grow again until the early summer, depending on how cold a winter there has been.

Although *Salvia patens* with its wonderful royal blue flowers will bloom in summer, it does also flower freely in early autumn. This salvia can be grown from seed in spring and treated like an annual. *Salvia involucrata* 'Bethellii', a tall plant at 1.3 m (4½ ft), has bright pink flowers which are covered pink bracts when in bud. *S. uliginosa* is another tall plant, which produces bright blue flowers on thin stems; it is best grown with other perennials such as Michaelmas daisies.

LATE AUTUMN-FLOWERING PERENNIALS

Dendranthemums (chrysanthemums)

No old cottage garden would have been complete without late-flowering perennials like dendranthemums (still widely known as chrysanthemums), which were often grown specially to provide cut flowers from late summer through to late autumn. There is such a variety of different

The large white blooms of *Anemone* 'Honorine Jobert' deserve a place in every cottage garden.

kinds of dendranthemums and many are very hardy, like pompons, spray or single cottage garden types, which can all be grown outdoors all the year round. Many of the old varieties are vigorous growers and soon make large clumps which need to be divided every two years or so. If this is not done the centre of the plant becomes old and woody and there are not so many flowers.

Dendranthemum 'Antastasia' is a rosy pink pompon variety 60 cm (24 in) tall; *D. rubellum* 'Clara Curtis' has single pink flowers with a yellow centre and grows to a height of 90 cm (36 in); *D. rubellum* 'Mary Stoker' has single flowers of a soft apricot-pink colour with a yellow centre, also growing to 90 cm (36 in); and *D.* 'Cottage Apricot' is a late-blooming variety with reddish-apricot flowers, whose petals shade to deep cream nearest the yellow centre.

All the above are very hardy, easy-to-grow dendranthemums, the only problem being that the flowers will sometimes be caught by frost. Protect with paper bags to avoid this.

Michaelmas daisies

Michaelmas daisies are probably the most widely grown autumn-flowering perennials and in nearly every garden there is likely to be at least one or two clumps of them creating bold splashes of colour for many weeks in autumn. Some of the older varieties grow just like a weed so care needs to be taken in selecting the right position for them. Other varieties are not so vigorous and are more suitable for small gardens where space is limited. Late autumn-flowering varieties include *Aster novae-angliae* 'Alma Potschke' with bright shocking pink flowers and growing to 1.06m (3½ ft); *A. novi-belgii* 'Carnival' that has semi-double deep cherry red flowers, growing to 45 cm (18 in); and *A. erocoïdes* 'White Heather', which produces branching stems of tiny white flowers that look like heather, is one of the very latest to bloom, and grows to 75 cm (30 in). All these varieties seem resistant to mildew.

FRAGRANT PERENNIALS

Fragrance has always been an important factor in a cottage garden border (Fig. 6); many believe scented flowers were originally grown to disguise the unsavoury smells of nearby pig sties and cow stalls. Nowadays we like the sweet scents of lily of the valley, sweet rocket and border carnations to drift across the garden, especially on warm sunny days when one is sitting out of doors.

Carnations

It is a pity that border carnations seem to have gone out of fashion in favour of the many varieties of modern pinks. However they can still be obtained from any of the many nurseries specializing in pinks and carnations. Good varieties to grow in the cottage garden border include *Dianthus* 'Aldridge Yellow', with semi-double yellow flowers; *D.* 'Bookham Perfume' that has beautifully scented semi-double crimson flowers; *D.* 'Eva Humphries' with semi-double pure white flowers, thinly edged with purple; and *D.* 'Forest Treasure' with double white flowers outlined and tinged with reddish mauve. These carnations bloom in the middle of the summer and provide an excellent cut flower. They grow best in a well-drained, slightly alkaline soil and a sunny position.

▲ This planting of autumn-flowering perennials includes *Dendranthemum* 'White Gloss', *Sedum*, 'September Glow', *Aster amellus* 'King George' and *Anemone* 'Prinz Heinrich'.

▶ The sweetly scented *Paeonia* 'Bowl of Beauty' is an excellent choice for the mixed border.

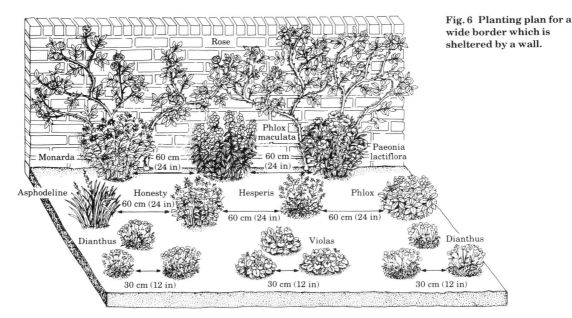

Rose

Phlox maculata

Paeonia lactiflora

Monarda · 60 cm (24 in) · 60 cm (24 in)

Asphodeline

Honesty 60 cm (24 in)

Hesperis 60 cm (24 in)

Phlox 60 cm (24 in)

Dianthus

Violas

Dianthus

30 cm (12 in)   30 cm (12 in)   30 cm (12 in)

Lily of the valley

Out of the many scented old cottage perennials grown, lily of the valley (*Convallaria majalis*) must be one of the favourites. It should be planted in half shade, and it is not fussy about soil condition as long as it is not too dry or too wet, although it sometimes takes a couple of years to get properly established. If you are limited for space try the slow-spreading variety *Convallaria rosea*, with its dainty pale pink flowers. An even more striking plant is *Convallaria majalis* 'Albostriata', bearing white flowers with attractive green and white-striped foliage.

Peonies

Peonies are superb cottage-garden perennials and once established will produce large clumps that will bloom for several weeks during early summer. They look lovely grown in mixed borders when planted with old shrub roses, hardy geraniums and pinks. Many varieties of peonies have sweetly scented flowers, and among the best is *Paeonia* 'Auguste Dessert' with semi-double

bright pink flowers that fade at the edges of the petals, height 75 cm (30 in). *P.* 'Bowl of Beauty', an anemone-centred peony, has fragrant pink blooms with a creamy centre and is one of the easiest and widely grown peonies, height 90 cm (3 ft). *P.* 'Sarah Bernhardt' is a vigorous plant growing 1.06 m (3½ ft) tall once well established; it produces large double, scented, pale pink blooms during the summer.

Peonies need rich, well-drained soil in sun, but will tolerate slight shade. They do not like disturbance, growing happily in the same place for many years providing they are well fed in the autumn. A mulch of well-rotted manure is best, although bone-meal can also be used.

It is most important to keep the plants moist once the buds start to form, as often the buds will fail to mature if kept too dry. Another problem is that the buds are sometimes damaged by late frosts. If a frost warning is given you can cover the plant with fibre fleece, which is a fine light material that can be tied around the plant to help protect it.

· 4 ·
Annuals and Biennials

Annuals and biennials have always been included in old cottage gardens grown in small patches between perennials or in lines in the vegetable garden. Many of these plants were grown to be used as cut flowers for indoors, especially fragrant annuals like sweet peas or biennial sweet williams, which also helped to brighten the small cottage rooms. Even during the winter months, when there was a lack of fresh flowers to pick, cottages always had available annuals like statice and helichrysum which they could harvest and dry.

HARDY ANNUALS

Hardy annuals are extremely easy to grow and nowadays can be used to great effect in a variety of ways. For example, they can be grown in lines in the vegetable garden and look lovely planted as an edging, making the vegetables look more attractive. Annuals such as cornflowers, godetia, larkspur and calendulas, which are useful as cut flowers, are best grown in this way as it is a pity to spoil a colourful border by picking too many of the flowers.

The seeds of hardy annuals can be directly sown in the position where you want them to grow in the spring, although it does depend on the weather. Do not sow seeds if the soil is very wet or frosty. If you like, you can also sow the seeds in early autumn, in a place where your garden is fairly sheltered, and before winter comes you should have some strong seedlings which will overwinter well. These seedlings will flower earlier than the spring-sown ones.

Hardy annuals like to grow in a sunny position and in almost any type of soil as long as it is not too wet. They are very good for filling any gaps between perennials in newly planted herbaceous borders. Again the seed can be sown directly in the spot where you want the annuals to blooms, which is a very simple way to add extra summer colours to new borders (Fig. 7).

From the vast range of easy-to-grow hardy annuals a gardener has to choose from, the following selection will give you colour from either flowers or seed heads throughout the summer months. These often continue into autumn, only ending when they are cut down by frosts or if they rot due to very wet, cold weather.

Agrostemma 'Milas'
This variety has bright pink flowers on fairly tall stems 90 cm (3 ft) long, and it will need some support while growing.

Candytuft
This is an old favourite which has been grown in cottage gardens for a great many years. It likes to grow in a sunny position and will tolerate poor soil. A neat compact plant, suitable for the edge of a border, it produces dense heads of small pink,

mauve or white flowers during early summer. Candytuft is an ideal annual to allow to self seed, but it is important to be able to recognize the seedlings when they are very small, because it is all too easy to mistake them for weeds and pull them up.

Clarkia

This is a very reliable hardy annual, blooming all summer and into autumn, and growing to about 45 cm (18 in) tall. Seeds are usually sold in packets of mixed colours; most of the flowers will be doubles and colours will range from pink, mauve, lavender and white.

Larkspur

If you want a taller annual, larkspur is very suitable as there are several tall varieties to choose from. *Larkspur* 'Giant Imperial Mixed' will produce delphinium-like 90 cm (3 ft) tall spikes of beautiful mauve, lavender, blue or pink flowers in early summer. Even more lovely is *Larkspur* 'Hyacinth Flowered Mixed', which has spikes of closely packed double flowers in colours of blue, pink, mauve or white, height 90 cm (3 ft), and is good for planting between perennials. For exposed windy gardens *Larkspur* 'Dwarf Hyacinth Flowered Mixed' is more suitable as it only grows 45 cm (18 in) tall. Larkspur seed can be successfully sown in early autumn or in the spring.

Pot marigold

Calendula officinalis is an old cottage garden annual that will grow in most types of soil including dry poor ones. It produces bright single orange flowers throughout the summer months,

◀ The lovely Shirley poppies are well-loved cottage garden annuals.

especially if you take the time to deadhead the plant regularly; it grows quite vigorously. *Calendula* 'Fiesta Gitana' is a new variety of dwarf habit which produces double blooms in shades of orange or yellow.

Poppies (annual)

Out of all the hardy annuals, poppies must be one of the most widely planted and well-loved in cottage gardens. Originally it was the native poppy, *Papaver rhoeas*, that was grown in gardens, the seeds of which were probably collected from surrounding cornfields where poppies grew in abundance and then scattered amongst other annuals in the garden. Poppies always self-seed freely and once introduced will soon disperse throughout a garden.

Poppies like to grow in a sunny position in a reasonable soil that is not too wet. The bright red flowers look wonderful on a summer day when poppies are thickly planted, and the flowers are followed by good seed heads which can be cut and dried for use in winter. Sow poppy seed directly in place where you want them to grow.

Annual poppies come in many shapes and colours but some of the loveliest are *P. rhoeas* 'Shirley Flowered Double Mixed'. These beautiful double poppies come in shades of red, orange, salmon and white, some with edgings of white, and they are all free-flowering for many weeks during the summer, height 60 cm (24 in). If you do not like double flowers try growing *P. rhoeas* 'Angel Wings Mixed' which includes many pastel shades of single poppies and some that will have bicolour flowers, growing to 30 cm (12 in).

There are many varieties of opium poppy (*Papaver somniferum*), including ones with single blooms and others with very double flowers that look like frilly balls. They usually grow to 90 cm (3 ft), the flowers come in colours of mauve, pink

37

or red and they have blue-green foliage that starts to die back when the large seed-pods appear (the seed-heads are good for drying).

Scarlet flax

Linum grandiflorum rubrum is a lovely graceful annual that has bright crimson flowers with a dark eye and grows to 30 cm (12 in). It likes a sunny position in well-drained soil and is very suitable for smaller gardens and for raised beds. Given the right weather conditions it will produce attractive small round seed-pods.

Cone flower

It is important to try and extend the flowering season of annuals and in order to do this plant the cone flower (*Rudbeckia hirta*) which will bloom during late summer and into the autumn. *Rudbeckia* 'Nutmeg' produces flowers in shades of orange and red, while *R.* 'Green Eyes' has deep yellow flowers with a green centre.

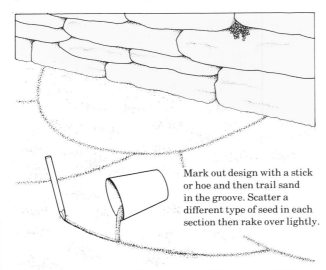

Mark out design with a stick or hoe and then trail sand in the groove. Scatter a different type of seed in each section then rake over lightly.

Fig. 7 Design for a directly sown annual border in which the seed is sown where it is to grow.

HALF-HARDY ANNUALS FOR CUT FLOWERS

Half-hardy annuals like asters and zinnias were great favourites as middle and late summer cottage-garden cut flowers. They are still very popular as the flowers are long lasting when picked for indoor use. The seeds can be sown in pans or boxes, under glass in spring, then pricked out into boxes a few weeks later as soon as the seedlings are large enough to handle. Plant out in the position where they are to grow when the risk of frost has passed.

Alternatively, the seed may be sown directly in the ground where they are to grow in early summer. Planting the seed this way does save you the trouble of bedding out although the plants will start to bloom about three weeks later than those started off under glass.

Asters

Asters should be grown in a sunny position in well-drained soil that is slightly alkaline; if you have an acid soil, add a little lime to it before planting.

The original asters had large single blooms, which were excellent for cutting. Some single varieties are still available today, including *Aster* 'Andrella' with large single blooms of blue, mauve, pink, red or white and a yellow centre. *A.* 'Ostrich Plume Mixed' is an old cottage garden favourite and long-lasting cut flower; it has large shaggy double flowers which come in shades of blue, lavender, pink and red.

New varieties come in many unusual shapes and sizes including *A.* 'Thunderball' which has thin spiky petals of deep red with dark green foliage, height 60 cm (24 in). *A.* 'Duchess' has large inviting double blooms that look rather like dendranthemums (see page 32), in colours of

EVERLASTING ANNUAL FLOWERS

Everlasting annual flowers such as statice, acroclinium, rhodanthe and helichrysum are grown specially to pick and dry for winter flower arrangements. Easy to grow in a well-drained sunny position, the seeds can either be sown in

yellow, red and pink, height 60 cm (24 in); it has stiff stems, which are good for cutting. If you have a small garden A. 'Dwarf Comet Mixed' would be suitable; it has large flowers but only grows to 25 cm (10 in) tall.

Zinnias

As young zinnias hate disturbance to their roots it is better to sow seeds where you want them to flower at the beginning of summer. They like to grow in fairly rich soil in a sunny position. They do not like damp weather and will sometimes rot off in these conditions, but even so they are certainly worth growing as they are a wonderful cut flower. The seeds can be sown individually in small pots in late spring and planted out when the risk of frosts are over. There will not be any damage to the new roots due to transplanting when grown like this.

Out of all the varieties *Zinnia elegans* 'Envy' is one of the most beautiful. It is 60 cm (24 in) tall, has greeny yellow flowers, makes an excellent long-lasting cut flower and is much loved by flower arrangers. *Z.* 'Dahlia-flowered Mixed' has very large flowers and grows 75 cm (2½ ft) tall, and *Z.* 'Persian Carpet' is a charming miniature with small double flowers in bright red, orange and yellow.

· ANNUALS FOR DRYING ·	
Name	**Description**
Acroclinium (*Helipterum roseum*)	Bright pink flowers with yellow centre
Bells of Ireland (*Molucella laevis*)	Tall spikes of tiny flowers with green bracts
Drumstick scabious (*Scabious stellata*)	Round bronze seed-heads on stiff stems
Hare's tail grass (*Lagurus ovatus*)	Soft fluffy white seed-heads
Lonas (*Lonas inodora* 'Goldrush')	Clusters of small round bright yellow flowers
Love-in-a-mist (*Nigella damascena* 'Miss Jekyll')	Seed-heads excellent for drying
Quaking grass (*Briza maxima*)	Small seed heads hang daintily on thin threads
Rhodanthe (*Helipterum manglesii*)	Pretty small pink or white flowers
Squirrel tail grass (*Hordeum jubatum*)	Silky feathery heads that gracefully droop
Statice (*Limonium*)	
● 'Sunset Mixed'	Tall everlasting flowers in shades of peach and apricot
● 'Special Mixed'	Tall stems of brightly coloured everlasting flowers
Strawflower (*Helichrysum*)	
●'Dwarf Mixed'	Compact plants of shiny brightly coloured flowers
● 'Hot Bikini'	Reddy orange flowers with yellow centre
Winged everlasting (*Ammobium alatum*)	Stems of small white flowers with golden centre

boxes or in the open ground where the plants are to bloom.

These everlasting annuals bloom throughout the summer. They should be picked for drying as soon as the flowers are fully out; if left too long before gathering they will shed their seeds when dry. Tie the flowers up in small bunches and hang upside down in a dry airy room until completely dried.

Grow zinnias in a sunny position where they will give you a colourful summer display.

BIENNIALS

The seeds of biennials are sown in summer, either in pans, boxes or in lines in a vegetable garden. When the seedlings are large enough to handle they can be transplanted into boxes or spaced out in open ground, ready to be moved into their flowering position in the autumn. The daisy *Bellis perennis* 'Pomponette' is grown as a biennial; it has very tight double daisy flowers in either pink, red or white and is useful at the edge of a border. The Canterbury bell (*Campanula media* 'Cup and Saucer Mixed') is a true cottage garden perennial which should be more widely grown. The large flowers that do indeed look like cups and saucers are produced on 75 cm (2½ ft) stems, with flowers in soft shades of pink, blue and lavender.

Forget-me-nots

Forget-me-nots (*Myosotis* species) are surely among the easiest biennials to grow from seed. Start them off either in boxes or the open ground and transplant where they are to bloom in early autumn. They will grow in almost any type of soil in sun or part shade.

There are many good varieties for spring bedding schemes, and they are ideal for planting with tulips. *Myosotis* 'Indigo' has deep blue flowers, but if you like to grow more unusual coloured forget-me-nots, try the variety 'Rose Pink' which has dainty pink flowers.

FRAGRANT ANNUALS AND BIENNIALS

Sweet peas

Lathyrus odoratus, among the best fragrant cut flowers, were grown in every cottage garden and have remained popular for over a hundred years. Many people grow sweet peas in a line in their vegetable garden trained up twigs, netting or canes, and this is the ideal place as the soil is usually well fed and therefore richer. They like to grow in the sun in a sheltered position as the wind will damage the blooms. In wet weather you will find that many of the buds drop off. To keep a succession of flowers they should be picked about every other day.

The seeds can be sown in small pots in autumn, then over-wintered in a cold frame, but beware of damage by slugs, snails and mice. Alternatively, they can be sown outdoors in spring. The old varieties are the most scented, 'Painted Lady' is very sweetly perfumed, the blooms being two shades of pink; if you want mixed colours 'Galaxy Mixed' has the most variety, free-flowering throughout the summer.

Sweet Williams

Dianthus barbatus blooms in early summer and is a superb biennial grown both for scent and as a cut-flower. It can be grown in the same way as wallflowers and needs similar conditions. Packets of seed usually include a mixture of colours.

Wallflowers

Wallflowers have always been grown in cottage gardens for spring fragrance and colour. They like a sunny position in free-draining soil that is slightly alkaline. Sow the seed in open ground in early summer, then transplant to where they are to flower in autumn.

They are very good for planting in containers mixed with tulips or narcissus. For the small garden the variety 'Dwarf Bedding Mixed' is very suitable, a mixture of bright yellow, red and orange colours, height 30 cm (12 in). For the larger garden the 'Harlequin' mixture is really outstanding; plants are vigorous in growth and there are pastel shades as well as the usual bright

Sweet William (*Dianthus barbatus*) is one of the most colourful biennials to grow for use as a cut flower.

red and orange colours, with flowers growing to 45 cm (18 in).

The flowers of the **tobacco plant** (*Nicotiana*) and **night-scented stock** (*Matthiola bicornia*) will fill the air with fragrance on warm summer evenings. These annuals should be grown near the house to give you the full benefit of their scent.

41

· 5 ·
Bulbs

Bulbs were always strongly featured in old cottage gardens, giving extra colour not only in spring but during summer and autumn as well. Bulbs and also corms were mixed with perennials in borders or grown in small beds mingled with spring-flowering bedding plants. Gladioli were among those specially grown in the vegetable gardens for their use as cut flowers. Under fruit trees in the garden or in small orchards, drifts of snowdrops would appear, to be followed a short time later by daffodils. How lovely they looked in spring under a canopy of apple blossom and fresh new leaves on the trees.

Naturalized bulbs

Bulbs that are naturalized under trees and shrubs can be left undisturbed for many years. They will soon multiply when grown this way, but it must be remembered that the old leaves and stems must not be cut off until they have withered and turned brown. If the leaves are cut off too soon, this will affect the flowering of the bulb the following year. Even today some people either bend over the daffodil tops or tie them tightly together to make them look tidy. But this is not a good thing to do as it stops the sap going back into the bulb which is necessary for producing healthy bulbs. Be patient, even though they will look untidy for a couple of weeks.

If the bulbs are planted under large mature trees, they sometimes tend to flower less and less, as the goodness in the soil is taken up by the tree rather than the bulb. If this happens sprinkle a little general fertilizer between the bulbs while they are still growing. This helps to feed the bulbs for next year.

SPRING-FLOWERING BULBS

Snowdrops

The snowdrop (*Galanthus nivalis*) will flower during the winter and early spring, regardless of snow or frosty weather. In fact it will bloom happily almost buried under snow with just the flower peeping through it. Snowdrops are very beautiful grown in drifts under trees or planted in groups in the lawn; the old leaves quickly die down and will have disappeared before the time comes to start mowing the lawn again in the spring.

Snowdrops will grow in sun or part shade and in any type of soil as long as it is not waterlogged during the winter. When first trying to establish them in a garden, plant them in groups of five or ten, with the bulbs quite close together. You can do this in the autumn, but they will naturalize far quicker when planted 'in the green', that is, with leaves growing out of the bulb in late spring.

Galanthus nivalis, the single-flowered snowdrop, is by far the most reliable and commonly grown variety, and it will soon multiply given the right conditions. *G. nivalis* 'Flore Pleno' has lovely double white flowers, with inner petals edged with green; they usually bloom slightly later than the single variety. *G.* 'Sam Arnott' has large, almost bell-shaped flowers that have green markings on the inner petals; it is lovely grown in raised beds where the full beauty of the bloom can be more easily seen.

Daffodils

Spring for most people means the wonderful sight of drifts of blooming golden daffodils, always so welcome after long wet and cold winters. They come in many sizes and colours, from the dainty early-flowering miniature narcissus to the large-flowered trumpet daffodils. Flowers are usually yellow or white in colour, but some varieties of daffodils have pink, red, orange and even green-edged trumpets. These are not to everyone's taste, as many people prefer the old-fashioned varieties.

Daffodils can be planted in all kinds of situations in sun or half shade and will grow in any type of soil. They should be planted as early as possible in the autumn. In herbaceous borders they are best planted in groups of three or five between the perennials, to give colour early in the season. They can be used with great success in spring bedding schemes grown between the winter and spring-flowering pansies, coloured primroses, forget-me-nots or wallflowers. They will grow happily under trees (but not conifers) shrubs or grass banks and can be naturalized in the lawn. Narcissus are excellent for planting in large and small containers.

With such an enormous number of narcissus to choose from it is quite difficult to select just a few good reliable varieties and species that will bloom at different times in the spring. Here are just a few that will give you a succession of flowering from late winter through to late spring.

Early-flowering varieties: *Narcissus* 'February Gold', an old variety of small trumpet daffodil, blooms all yellow and is one of the earliest to bloom – often in late winter – it grows to 30 cm (12 in). *N.* 'Peeping Tom' is a tall yellow daffodil

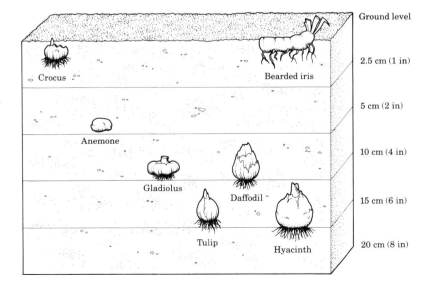

Fig. 8 Planting depth for bulbs and corms, which is usually two or three times the depth of the bulb or corm.

Ground level

Crocus   Bearded iris   2.5 cm (1 in)

5 cm (2 in)

Anemone   10 cm (4 in)

Gladiolus   Daffodil   15 cm (6 in)

Tulip   Hyacinth   20 cm (8 in)

with a long narrow trumpet; very long lasting, it will be in bloom for many weeks and is not affected by adverse weather conditions; height 35 cm (14 in). Slightly more unusual is *N.* 'Telamonious Plenus', with double yellow flowers which are not usually spoilt by bad weather.

Mid-season varieties: *Narcissus* 'Birma' is a small cupped narcissus with bright yellow petals and a small orange-red trumpet, very free flowering. *N.* 'Barrett Browning' is an old reliable variety with pure white petals and an orange cup which is frilly. *N.* 'Mount Hood', one of the very best, is an all-white trumpet daffodil, which is slightly cream in colour when it first comes out

Snowdrops (*Galanthus nivalis*) in bloom herald the arrival of early spring and the taste of things to come.

and grows to 45 cm (18 in). *N.* 'Spellbinder' is a lovely trumpet daffodil with large sulphur yellow flowers, which gradually fade to an off-white.

Late-flowering varieties: *N.* 'White Lion' is a beautiful white-flowered double narcissus, with large petals, some of which are cream in colour. *N. cyclamineus* 'Lilac Charm' is a new variety with white reflexed petals and a long narrow pinky-lilac trumpet. An unusual narcissus, *N.* 'Sir Winston Churchill' is a tall multi-headed tazetta narcissus; it has double white flowers with some small orange petals mixed together in the centre, very fragrant and blooms in late spring. *N. jonquilla* 'Sun Disc' is one of the very latest of narcissus to bloom; it has small flowers with round gold petals and a flat tiny centre that looks like a gold medal.

Crocuses

Crocus corms really look best naturalized in drifts in the lawn (Fig. 9) or under deciduous trees. They need to be planted in groups of five or ten, in a position where they will get the sun for most of the day, otherwise the flowers will not open properly. They are not too fussy about soil conditions, although they will rot off if planted in very damp or wet places. Crocuses are suitable for growing in rockeries, raised beds and at the edge of a border.

Crocuses are very prone to damage by mice and voles in mild or wet winters. If you find small holes in the ground where you have planted crocuses, these can be a tell-tale sign that mice or voles have been digging down and that some corms may have been eaten. It is not an easy problem to overcome. You can put down traps baited with peanuts to catch them, but remember to put traps under a box or pot, otherwise you might catch a bird by mistake. Another old remedy to alleviate the problem was to put dried

Crocuses look wonderful on a sunny spring day but should be planted thickly.

Interesting effects can be created by mixing tulips with cowslips and hellebores.

holly leaves next to the corms when they were planted, with the idea that when the mouse or vole dug down to get the corms it would prick its nose and leave the corms alone. I have never tried this method but am told that it works. A third method is to soak string in paraffin or creosote and then push it under the ground with the corms or simply lay it on the surface in the hope that the smell will keep rodents away.

In the spring when crocus buds appear, they will often be eaten off at ground level by mice and voles, while birds will peck the petals, always eating the yellow-flowered varieties first. Squirrels and pheasants will also inflict damage on crocuses.

Winter-flowering varieties: *Crocus chrysanthus* 'Blue Pearl' will bloom sometimes in late winter or early spring, depending on how frosty the weather is. This crocus has beautiful pale blue flowers with a yellow centre. Another early-flowering variety is *C. chrysanthus fuscotinctus*, with yellow flowers which has plum-coloured stripes on the outside of the petals. *Crocus tommasinianus* 'Whitewell Purple' has violet-mauve flowers that have slightly pointed petals, is free-flowering and soon naturalizes.

Spring-flowering varieties: The large-flowered dutch crocuses bloom slightly later. They have much larger flowers and are very suitable for growing in lawns as the leaves die

45

down quite quickly after flowering. Some people like to plant mixed colours, but I think it's better to plant in groups of all one colour. There are several named varieties of this type of crocus, including 'Little Dorrit' that has pale lilac flowers, 'Pickwick', again pale lilac but with dark mauve stripes, and 'Snowstorm' which has pure white, almost globe-shaped flowers.

· SPRING-FLOWERING BULBS FOR NATURALIZING ·

Name	Description
Bluebell (*Hyacinthoïudes non-scripta*	Arching stems of bluebell-shaped flowers; good under trees
Crocus	
• *C. chrysanthus* 'Cream Beauty'	Cream flowers with bright orange stamens
• *C. tommasinianus*	Pinkish mauve flowers; very free flowering
Daffodil	
• *Narcissus* 'Ice Follies'	White petals with wide pale yellow cup
• *Narcissus* 'Sempre Avanti'	Cream petals with wide bright orange cup
Glory-of-the-snow (*Chionodoxa gigantea*)	Large mauvish blue flowers with white centre
Old pheasant's eye (*Narcissus poeticus* var. *recurvus*)	Pure white flowers with bright eye; very fragrant
Snowdrop (*Galanthus nivalis*)	Single flowers; blooms from late winter onwards
Squill (*Scilla siberica* 'Spring Beauty')	Short spikes of bright blue flowers
Striped squill (*Puschkinia libanotica*)	Pale blue flowers with darker stripe in centre of petals
Winter aconite (*Eranthus cilicica*)	Bright yellow flowers with cut-leafed foliage
Wind flower (*Anemone blanda* 'White Splendour')	Large pure white flowers; very long lasting
Wood anemone (*Anemone nemorosa*)	Dainty white flowers; likes a shady position

Tulips

Tulips are a very old cottage-garden bulb; they have been grown in cottage gardens for well over a hundred years, usually mixed with other bulbs and perennials in sunny beds and borders. Many of the old varieties had striped petals which were certainly eye-catching when in bloom. Others, like the late spring-flowering cottage tulips, come in many different colours; and the fringed parrot tulips are very unusual, but not everyone's choice of bulb. Tulips have a very long flowering season beginning in early spring with the dwarf *Kaufmanniana* varieties, and continuing with early double ones and finally into late spring and early summer with cottage and lily-flowered tulips.

Tulips like to grow in a sunny well-drained position otherwise they will not bloom properly. Do not plant tulips until late autumn; if planted too early they will suffer from diseases. They can be planted in groups in beds and borders or between spring-flowering bedding plants like wallflowers, polyanthus, pansies or forget-me-nots.

Early spring-flowering varieties: *Tulipa kaufmanniana* 'Johann Strauss' is a dwarf tulip with creamy white flowers, with petals that have a wide red stripe on the outside and good dark green striped foliage. *T. kaufmanniana* 'Shakespeare' has lovely apricot blooms with attractive striped foliage and *T. fosteriana* 'Cantata' has bright scarlet flowers with broad glossy green leaves.

Mid-season-flowering varieties: *Tulipa greigii* 'Toronto' has pretty orange apricot flowers and is a multi-headed variety with several blooms on one stem. *T.* 'Fringed Beauty' is an unusual early double tulip: it has orange-red flowers with a fringed edge of yellow. *T.* 'Carnival de Nice' is an unusual double paeony-flowered tulip that has white flowers with red stripes and splashes; it looks like an old variety of Rembrandt tulip.

Late-flowering varieties: *T.* 'Clara Butt' is an old tall variety of cottage tulip that has lovely pink flowers with a white stripe. *T.* 'Queen of Bartigons' is a beautiful salmon pink cottage tulip, very reliable and long lasting. *T.* 'Ballerina' is a tall orange-flushed yellow lily-flowered tulip, that has long spiky petals; it looks lovely planted with orange wallflowers. Lastly, *T.* 'Orange Favourite' is an outstanding fringed orange parrot tulip with green blotches on the petals.

SUMMER-FLOWERING BULBS

You should be able to have bulbs or corms in flower in nearly every month of the year in your garden. After the tulips have finished, alliums, summer-flowering anemones and ornithogalums will be blooming, to be followed by gladioli and lilies (more about lilies on page 50). Most summer-flowering bulbs like to grow in a sunny well-drained position and are suitable for planting between perennials like geraniums, penstemons, phlox and pinks.

Alliums
Although not really thought of as an old cottage-garden plant, alliums (ornamental onion) are now very useful for helping to create a cottage garden

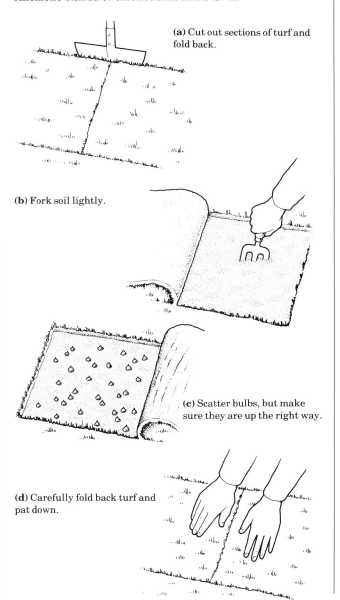

Fig. 9 An easy way of planting small bulbs like crocuses, *Anemone blanda* or chionodoxas in the lawn.

(a) Cut out sections of turf and fold back.

(b) Fork soil lightly.

(c) Scatter bulbs, but make sure they are up the right way.

(d) Carefully fold back turf and pat down.

effect when mixed with perennials in beds and borders. Most varieties of alliums prefer well-drained soil in a sunny position; once established they will increase readily by self-seeding. The seedling usually take two to three years for the bulbs to reach flowering size.

One of the most beautiful is *Allium carinatum pulchellum*, which produces heads of small pinky mauve nodding flowers and grows to 37 cm (15 in). It hardly has any leaves and they tend to die away before flowering. Useful for planting between low-growing perennials, like pinks, *Campanula carpatica* and *Ajuga reptans* 'Burgundy Glow'. *Allium carinatum pulchellum album* has lovely white nodding flowers and is very good grown with *Gysophila repans* 'Rosea'. These alliums will bloom for about two months during the middle of the summer, and are a favourite flower of bumble bees.

The drumstick allium (*Allium sphaerocephalon*) has compact heads of small reddish-purple flowers on stiff stems, 45 cm (18 in) high; a long-lasting flower, it is excellent for picking and drying for winter arrangements.

Allium flavum is a charming, pale yellow-flowered allium, blooming in mid-summer, height 30 cm (12 in). It is suitable for smaller gardens and raised beds in a sunny position.

Plant allium bulbs in early autumn. They are obtainable from good garden centres at that time of the year or you can order them from one of the many mail-order bulb catalogues.

◄ **Alliums can be grown most successfully planted between perennials in a border. After flowering has finished, the seed heads can be cut and used in dried flower arrangements.**

▶ *Gladiolus byzantinus* **looks best when planted with hardy geraniums and astrantia. This is a fully hardy species that can be left in the ground throughout the winter.**

Star of Bethlehem
Ornithogalum umbellatum is a lovely dwarf bulb for planting on the edge of a sunny border in well-drained soil. It has white starry flowers that open wide when the sun is out and will bloom in early summer. The bulbs need to be planted fairly close together in groups of five or ten.

Gladioli
The large-flowered gladioli were mainly grown in lines in the vegetable garden to use as cut flowers. They seem to be happier planted in this way rather than competing with perennials in a border. The corms of the large-flowered gladioli can be planted in early spring, but not if the weather is frosty or very wet. To extend the flowering season do not put all the corms in at

49

once but plant a few about every two weeks until late spring. That way you will get a succession of flowers from summer through to early autumn. Having such large flowers on tall stems does tend to make the plant top-heavy and you will find that they need to be staked.

There are many named varieties to choose from; some are brightly coloured, like *Gladiolus* 'Trader Horn', which has large scarlet blooms with a white throat, and *G.* 'Esta Bonita' that has orangy yellow flowers with a darker centre.

Gladiolus byzantinus has smaller flowers of reddy mauve and is suitable for growing in a herbaceous border. It looks attractive mixed with old-fashioned columbines as they both bloom in early summer. The corms of this gladiolus are planted in the autumn and they can be allowed to naturalize. There is no need to dig them up as you would large-flowered varieties.

AUTUMN-FLOWERING BULBS

Autumn-flowering bulbs are grown far more widely today than they once were. But in most old cottage gardens there were always a few autumn-flowering crocuses and a few *Cyclamen hederifolium*. There was also usually a large clump of Guernsey lily (*Nerine bowdenii*), an excellent long-lasting cut flower.

FRAGRANT BULBS

Hyacinths

Hyacinths must be one of the most fragrant bulbs grown; they are lovely when planted in bowls for indoor use, but equally good for using in spring bedding displays in borders or containers. They look quite stunning when grown closely together in formal bedding schemes. The bulbs should be planted 15 cm (6 in) apart for this kind of display.

The scent from hyacinths is wonderful on a warm spring day and will drift all round your garden.

When it comes to selecting varieties for outdoor planting, you cannot beat the old favourites like *Hyacinthus* 'Delft Blue' that will produce a large head of beautiful blue flowers which are not affected by rain or frost; *H.* 'Lady Derby' with lovely pink flowers on strong stems that bloom in early spring; and *H.* 'City of Haarlem' which has pale yellow blooms (this hyacinth usually flowers about a week later than the other two varieties).

Lilies

Lilies (Fig. 10) were always a feature in old cottage gardens, especially the beautiful Madonna lily (*Lilium candidum*). If the cottage had small borders by the front door, this was where the lilies were sometimes grown so that the fragrance of the blooms would drift indoors. The wall of the cottage would also give the lily some protection from strong winds.

Fig. 10 **Planting lily bulbs. Some types of lilies are planted much deeper than others.**

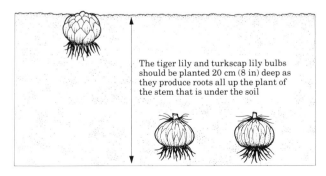

The Madonna lily is planted at soil surface level

The tiger lily and turkscap lily bulbs should be planted 20 cm (8 in) deep as they produce roots all up the plant of the stem that is under the soil

· 6 ·

Vegetables and Herbs

The growing of vegetables was the first priority in old cottage gardens and flowers always came second, planted where there was any available space left. The cottagers had to grow enough vegetables to feed their families all through the year. This meant not only growing plenty of fresh vegetables like peas, broad beans, runner beans, marrows and lettuce for use during spring and summer, but also growing sufficient vegetables that could be stored for use in the winter months. This is a task that people today hardly ever bother with as it is so easy to freeze excess crops.

VEGETABLES

Storing vegetables

Cottagers had many different ways of storing vegetables, all of which worked very well; it does seem a pity that some methods they used are not continued today. They would grow row upon row of potatoes, carrots, beetroot and parsnips to lift and store in clamps in the garden. Or if there was a shed or outhouse, carrots, beetroot and parsnips could also be stored in large wooden boxes in between layers of dry sand. I can remember doing this about 15 years ago; it does seem to work very well and the vegetables stayed in good condition until the spring. Other ways of storing vegetables are either to pickle them or make chutney, and also to salt runner beans. I can remember the beans were sliced and put in large glazed earthen-ware jars between layers of salt. This method does not get used today.

The storing of onions and shallots has not changed over the years. We still lay them out to dry and once they have ripened off they can be kept in nets or strung up. These can then be stored in a cool airy place and should be checked now and then to make sure none have rotted.

Growing methods

Vegetable gardens can be any size: this will depend a lot on how many people there are in the family and also how much space you have for growing vegetables. Many people still prefer the traditional way of growing vegetables in large plots. These plots are 10 m (30 ft) or so wide and may vary in length from 15.25–27.5 m (50–90 ft). By having a large plot you will be able to follow a three-year feeding rotation plan: in the first year the ground should be manured, in the second year it should be fertilized and limed, and in the third it should be just fertilized.

One of the best ways to grow vegetables is to have 1.2 m (4 ft) wide beds with a path either side (the beds can be as long as you like). By having narrow beds you do not have to tread on the soil very much as the vegetables can be reached from either side. Ideally you should have at least three beds so that the crops can be properly rotated; this is a very essential part of vegetable gardening to help protect crops from pests and diseases.

Choosing a suitable site

You may already have a vegetable garden, but if you are starting from scratch choose a sunny, fairly open position, away from any large mature trees. It should have some shelter from winds, especially those from the north east. The shelter can be provided by hedges, fences or walls. Hedges should be about 1.5 m (5 ft) away, otherwise all the goodness from the vegetable plot will be taken away by their roots. Fences or walls are better and will allow certain fruits and vegetables to be trained against them. Do not choose a wet boggy site as vegetables do not like to grow in waterlogged soil; their roots are likely to rot off during autumn and winter if planted in these conditions. Wet ground can be improved by installing drainage pipes; this is a hard task but worth doing in the long run. Poor soil is soon remedied by a regular programme of feeding.

PREPARATION OF THE SOIL

The preparation of the soil will affect how well the vegetables grow. You may be lucky to have an old cottage garden with a good depth of fertile soil; this comes with years of working and feeding the ground. All too often, however, a gardener is faced with an overgrown weedy site, full of perennial weeds that are difficult to get rid of.

Clearing perennial weeds from the soil

It is worth taking time to eradicate perennial weeds from the soil before starting a planting programme. This can be done in various ways depending on how much time you have to spare for working on the ground. The easiest way is to use weedkiller on the affected areas. Use one that contains glyphosate if you want to cultivate the ground after the weeds are dead. This chemical acts through the foliage and is translocated into the roots, killing them. Some very persistent weeds will need two sprayings.

If you do not like using chemicals in the garden, the next best way is to cover the soil for a couple of months with black polythene or an old carpet; this does not look very elegant but will bring the roots of perennial weeds to the surface. After about six weeks roll back the covering and you should be able to remove the roots quite easily. Recover and repeat when necessary until all the roots have been removed. Some weeds, such as nettles and docks, can be forked out without the need to cover them first.

Once these persistent weeds have been removed, the ground will be ready for digging (Fig. 11).

Digging

If possible dig over the ground in the autumn as this will allow time for it to lay fallow and be broken down with the frost and rain during the winter months.

When digging the ground over for the first time after years of neglect, one should double dig the soil to help to improve the structure of it (see Fig. 12). Where the soil is poor or very free-draining, dig in some well-rotted manure, spent mushroom compost or your own rotted-down compost. This will add organic matter to the soil and will help to stop the soil from drying out in hot, dry weather.

It will take a few years to build up a good depth of fertile soil but it is well worth the effort.

● *Chalk soils* If your garden is on solid chalk and you want to grow vegetables, the best way to do this is to grow them in raised beds. Do not dig up the chalk but keep applying thick mulches of well-rotted compost or manure, which will soon rot down when lightly forked into the top surface of the chalk. You will eventually create excellent growing conditions for the vegetables. Brick, concrete blocks or old railway sleepers are just some of the many materials that can be used for making a low retaining wall round these raised beds. Once made, these beds are easy to maintain but they must be mulched regularly as the goodness in the soil is soon leached away.

● *Wet heavy soils* Conditions are hardly every perfect in a garden and if it's not too dry, then it's often too wet or waterlogged. Drainage pipes can be laid underground to remove excess water from it, but remember to dig a soakaway to take the drainage water away from the vegetable plot, otherwise you will find that you have created a bog.

Another way of draining wet areas is to put a layer of coarse gravel at the bottom of the trench when you are digging over the ground to a spade's depth.

● *Clay soils* In clay soils you will get the same wet conditions at certain times of the year, to be followed by months when the clay bakes and cracks appear in the ground during dry weather. If you have this type of soil and have experienced these problems, not only do you need the layer of coarse gravel underneath but you should fork gravel or grit into the soil as well. Other materials for lightening the soil include forest bark, straw, spent mushroom compost and leafmould. Well-rotted manure is excellent to use for this purpose as not only does it help break down the clay but it will add nutrients to the soil. If possible, only use manure that has been well rotted because you may have a problem of weed seeds germinating if the manure is too fresh. It is a pity to re-introduce weeds once you have cleared your ground. Fresh manure should be stacked for at least six months before using it.

When spring comes it is easy just to rake the ground over ready for sowing and planting.

Vegetable gardens can be made more ornamental by an edging of parsley or annual flowers.

TYPES OF VEGETABLES

If you have a large vegetable garden you will be able to grow a great range of vegetables and also have room for some of the perennials, such as rhubarb, asparagus, jerusalem artichokes and globe artichokes. If you are fairly limited for space, be selective in the kind of vegetables you grow. Always find space for salad vegetables as they are delicious freshly picked and eaten. Grow ones that do not take up a lot of space; onions, shallots, beetroot and carrots, for example, can be planted close together. You will be surprised how big a crop you will harvest given good growing conditions.

The growing of root and tuberous crops was all-

53

Fig. 11 Single digging, where a good trench is dug out first before digging commences.

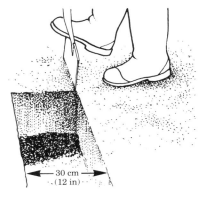

(a) Dig out a trench 25 cm (10 in) deep and put soil in a heap at the point where the digging will finish. This is to fill in the final trench.

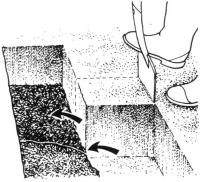

(b) Working backwards, dig the soil and place it in the front trench. Manure can be put in the trench first and then covered over.

important to cottagers, as it provided a diverse selection of vegetables for use in the kitchen during summer, autumn and winter. They grew rows and rows of potatoes, carrots, beetroots, parsnips and turnips, and all these vegetables were used for stews, casseroles or making soup. In addition, the peelings from the vegetables were boiled up and fed to pigs and chickens.

These vegetables are simple to grow given the right type of soil and situation. Some do not want well-manured soil which can create forked roots on carrots and parsnips instead of one long straight one.

Beans, broad
Beans and peas (see page 57) like moisture-retentive soil that has been well manured the previous autumn. In favourable districts they can be sown in the autumn, otherwise wait until early spring. Both need plenty of water during their growing season.

Broad beans can be sown in the autumn in favourable sites, and the best variety for this purpose is 'Aquadula'. In colder areas sow the seed in early spring for cropping in early summer. Plant the seed 4 cm (1¼ in) deep and 20 cm (8 in) apart. Pinch out the growing tips when the plant is fully grown, as this will stop the plants being infested with black fly.

Beans, runner
Runner beans should be grown in deep well-manured soil. The seed can be planted outdoors where they are to grow when the risk of frosts are over or the seed can be started off in pots and planted out in early summer. They require plenty of water during dry spells in order to produce a heavy crop.

Runner beans can be supported in several ways, including using hazel poles in two lines that are crossed over and tied at the top. Alternatively, four strong poles can be positioned in a square and tied at the top.

Beet
Sow beetroot seed in drills in late spring (any earlier and some varieties are likely to bolt and run up to seed). Beetroot like the same soil

· HANDY TIP ·

After you have removed the old broad bean or pea plants after harvesting their crop, sow rows of turnips in their place. Sow the seed thickly, and when it is fully grown, the plants can be dug into the ground as green manure.

Fig. 12 Double digging, where the trench is dug out to the depth of two spits first.

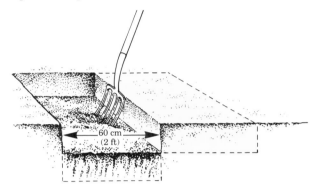

(a) Dig out a trench 60 cm (24 in) wide, fork over the bottom and then cover with manure or rotted compost.

(b) Dig out and put soil in front, covering the manure.

conditions as carrots (see below). Thin out the seedlings when big enough to handle. You can start pulling them when they are a little bigger than a golf ball. Beetroot have a better flavour and are more tender when used small. Excess crop can be picked, frozen or stored in dry sand.

'Boltardy' is a variety resistant to bolting and is globe shaped; 'Forono' has long tapering roots; and more unusual is 'Burpee's Golden' with yellow roots.

Brassicas

No kitchen garden is complete without brassicas, which include cabbage, cauliflowers, sprouts and calabrese. There are different varieties for growing at different times of the year. The seeds of cauliflowers and cabbage can be sown under glass in early spring; the seedlings then planted outdoors in late spring. The seeds of all types of brassicas can be sown outdoors from late spring onward. The seedlings should be spaced 45 cm (18 in) apart, then put a collar around the base of the stem to keep away the cabbage root fly. Give the plants plenty of water in dry weather. The cauliflowers 'Snowball' and 'All the Year Round' are both reliable, early-maturing varieties.

Carrots

Carrots like to be grown in light fertile soil that does not have many stones in it, otherwise some of the carrots will be misshapen. For very early carrot crops sow the seed in frames or under cloches in late winter and the carrots should be ready for pulling from early summer onwards. 'Amsterdam Forcing' and 'Early Nantes' are both suitable for growing in frames or under cloches.

Begin sowing carrot seed outdoors in spring for summer harvesting. Sow the seed fairly thickly, as it germinates better this way than when it is

Runner beans look attractive when trained up a frame or poles and will help to hide a shed or fence.

sparsely sown. Sow in shallow drills and sprinkle granules of chlorpyrifos or diazinon over the seed to keep the carrot fly away. If you don't like to use chemicals in the garden, try the following alternative method, which is to grow your carrots between rows of onions or shallots. The onion smell will stop the flies from finding the carrots, though you must remember to put onions on the ends of the rows of carrots and not just either side. This idea has been used quite successfully for a great many years.

Once the seed has germinated, thin out the seedlings so that the carrots are about 5 cm (2 in) apart. Keep the weeds under control by carefully hand weeding.

Today carrots come in many shapes and sizes, from the tiny round 'Parmec' to 'St Valery', which is a long tapering carrot. They can be grown in any size garden as they do not take up much space. They even look attractive grown in small patches between annual flowers.

Leeks

Leeks were always grown in old cottage gardens and today they are just as popular as they will provide you with a fresh vegetable throughout the winter months. Leeks are very hardy and will tolerate very frosty weather. Even in a smaller garden it is worth growing just a few.

Outside sow seed in mid-spring in drills and space out in late spring where leeks are to grow.

Onions

Onions can be grown in two different ways, one is from seed and the other from sets. You can get good results using either method, but growing onions from sets is much easier.

Onion seed can be sown in drills in late summer and the small onion seedlings transplanted in early spring to where they are to grow, or the young plants can be just thinned out to 15 cm (6 in) apart. Not all varieties of onions are suitable for growing this way, so do read the instructions on the seed packet carefully before planting. If you want to grow large onions, sow the seed under glass in the middle of the winter; when the seedlings each have two leaves they can be pricked out in deep boxes or potted up individually in 7.5 cm (3 in) pots. Plant out in early spring in ground that was manured the previous autumn. Apply water when necessary during dry weather. By the middle of summer they can be lifted and dried ready for storing for winter use. Good varieties to grow from seed are 'Bedfordshire Champion', 'Ailsa Craig' and 'James Long Keeping'.

Growing onions from sets is very simple, just rake over the ground in early spring and push the small bulbs into the soil so that just the tops of the bulbs can be seen. Plant 15 cm (6 in) apart and 30 cm (12 in) between the rows. Do not plant the sets in very wet or frosty weather. Once the sets start to grow, cultivate the same way as onions grown from seed.

Parsnips

Parsnips will grow in the same conditions as carrots but must have a good depth of soil in order to grow really successfully. Do not sow the seed too early if the ground is wet and cold: late spring is best. Only use fresh seed as old seed does not germinate well. Thin out the seedlings to 10 cm (4 in) apart and allow 38 cm (15 in) between the rows. Grow varieties that are resistant to the disease parsnip canker such as 'Avonresister' and 'Gladiator'.

You can start harvesting parsnips in late summer, but many people prefer to leave them in the ground until there has been one or two frosts, as this will bring out the flavour more.

Peas

Peas can be sown in early spring in shallow trenches and then at fortnightly intervals until early summer for a succession of crops. 'Feltham First' is an early variety and will tolerate some frosts, and 'Hurst Greenshaft' matures later and is an excellent cropper and a good pea for freezing.

When the peas first come up they are very prone to damage by slugs and snails. Sometimes

A parsley hedge planted along the rows of peas is decorative as well as being a useful addition to the kitchen garden.

mice will dig down and eat the peas just as they are beginning to germinate. You may need to take precautions against this.

Peas need some kind of support while growing. Hazel twigs were always used and nowadays this is still the best method of support if you are able to obtain them.

Potatoes

Potatoes must be the most widely grown of all vegetables, not least because they are so versatile in the kitchen. They grow best in deep fertile soil and need regular watering in hot dry weather. The choice of varieties to grow is vast and will vary in flavour and texture; some varieties will produce a greater crop. Varieties of potatoes come under the headings of Early, Second Early and

Maincrop. If you live in an area that has a mild climate you can start your planting programme in early spring, using one of the early varieties of potatoes.

Start planting your potatoes in early spring if the weather conditions allow, but hold back for a while if it's very cold or the ground is water-logged. Plant the tubers 38 cm (15 in) apart and 75 cm (2½ ft) between the rows. Make 15 cm

(6 in) deep holes with a trowel and put a tuber in the hole with the eyes or short growths pointing upwards. Fill in the holes by raking over the soil. Earth up the plants when leaves start to appear.

The foliage is very prone to frost damage and should be covered with fibre fleece or plastic on nights when frosts may occur. Water when necessary, but weeding is not such a problem as the foliage of the potatoes will suppress many weeds. Watch out for slug and snail damage.

Start lifting your potatoes in summer, allowing them to dry before storing. Do not store ones that have holes or that have been damaged when forking them up.

Varieties to grow: *Early* – 'Maris Bard', a good white oval potato, and 'Arran Pilot'; *Second early* – 'Nadine', a good-shaped white potato, heavy cropper, and 'Wilja', a pale yellow oval potato; *Maincrop* – 'Desirée', one of the very best for flavour, red-skinned and long-keeping, and 'Maris Piper', a large potato producing a heavy crop.

Shallots

Many people prefer the milder flavour of shallots to onions (see page 56). They are handy to use in the kitchen when just a small amount of flavouring is required, as some onions are too large for that purpose. Another good reason for growing shallots is that they keep better than onions and last longer.

Shallots should be planted in early spring when the soil conditions are right (the ground must not be too wet or cold). To plant, just push the shallot into the soil the same as you would an onion set, but they should be spaced 30 cm (12 in) apart and 30 cm (12 in) between the rows. If you plant large shallots, they will divide and produce many smaller ones, but if you plant small ones they will produce just two or three large shallots which are

· RECOMMENDED VEGETABLE VARIETIES ·

Name	Description
Bean, broad 'Imperial Green Longpod'	Long pods of tender green beans
Bean, dwarf 'The Prince'	Long straight fleshy beans' crops well
Bean, runner 'Streamline'	A reliable variety, bearing a good crop of very long beans
Beetroot 'Detroit Crimson Globe'	Old variety of round beet with deep flesh
Broccoli 'Early Purple Sprouting'	Produces a succession of tender purple sprouts in winter
Brussel Sprouts 'Peer Gynt'	Tightly packed stems of medium-sized sprouts
Cabbage 'Mincole'	A compact hard-headed cabbage for autumn use
Leek 'Autumn Mammoth 2 – Argenta'	Long thick leeks with a mild flavour
Lettuce 'Lakeland'	Delicious crisp iceberg-type lettuce
Onion 'Ailsa Craig'	An old variety, producing large globe-shaped onions
Parsnip 'Hollow Crown Improved'	Long white roots for late summer and autumn use
Pea 'Onward'	Produces a heavy crop of large fat peas
Potato 'Desirée'	The best red potato with excellent flavour
Radish 'Cherry Belle'	Crisp round bright red radish
Turnip 'Model White'	A tender round white variety

the size of small onions. In wet weather slugs will sometimes eat shallots and it is advisable to use slug pellets or bait. Keep weed free and water when necessary. Shallots start to dry off in the middle of summer, sometimes earlier; they can then be lifted and put out on trays or boxes to dry. When completely dry, trim off some of the roots and tops, and store in shallow boxes in a cool place. Check from time to time and remove any that have rotted. The two best varieties to grow are 'Dutch Red', an excellent keeper, and 'Hative de Niort' which produces beautifully shaped shallots that are often the size of onions (a good variety for showing).

HERBS

Cottage gardens always contained a great assortment of herbs which were used for culinary and medicinal purposes. Many herbs look very ornamental and will fill the air with wonderful aromas on warm or hot days. Herbs can be grown in the vegetable garden; here parsley will make an attractive edging to the lines of vegetables. It is surprising how much stronger parsley grows in rich soil. Many herbs are very vigorous in growth and are better contained in specially partitioned formal herb gardens.

Herbs in the vegetable garden
Grow a border of perennial herbs at one end of your vegetable garden. Include sage, fennel, sweet Cicely and rosemary; this will create a lovely aromatic border of useful herbs. These herbs like to grow in a sunny position in free-draining soil. Gravel can be added to the soil before planting if the condition of the ground is wet or heavy clay.

To create an ornamental edging round the vegetable plots, plant parsley, basil, thyme and

· A SELECTION OF COTTAGE GARDEN HERBS ·

Name	Description
Basil (*Ocimum basilicum*)	A half-hardy annual for a sunny sheltered position
Bay (*Laurus nobilis*)	Hardy shrub with aromatic dark green, glossy leaves
Chamomile (*Chamaemelum nobile*)	A hardy mat-forming perennial with fine foliage
Chives (*Allium schoenoprasum*)	Hardy perennial with onion-tasting leaves
Dill (*Anethum graveolens*)	An annual with feathery leaves and aromatic seeds
Fennel (*Foeniculum vulgare*)	A tall perennial with lovely foliage
Lavender (*Lavendula angustifolia*)	Evergreen shrub with grey foliage and fragrant flowers
Mint (*Mentha spicata*)	An invasive hardy perennial with strongly scented foliage
Parsley (*Petroselinum crispum*)	For best crops grow as an annual
Rosemary (*Rosemarinus officinalis*)	Evergreen shrub with small thin leaves
Sage (*Salvia officinalis*)	An evergreen sub-shrub with grey-green foliage
Sweet Cicely (*Myrrhis odorata*)	Hardy perennial with fern-like foliage
Tarragon (*Artemisia dracunculus*)	A perennial herb which needs protection in winter
Thyme (*Thymus vulgaris*)	Low-growing evergreen sub-shrub with tiny leaves

chives. Parsley is the best for this purpose and when closely planted will look like a dwarf, bright green hedge. Grow parsley as an annual by sowing the seeds in lines where they are to grow in late spring. Do not put the seed in too early as it will often rot or be slow to germinate in wet and cold weather.

If you plant mint in the kitchen garden it will need to be contained as it is very invasive. Bury an old bucket that has some holes made in the bottom of it and then plant the mint roots in the bucket. This will help to stop the mint from spreading quickly.

Small formal herb gardens

Small formal herb gardens can be created by good use of bricks, paving slabs or stone. Any number of patterns and designs can be made with these materials, but the design should fit in with the rest of your garden. If possible herb gardens should be sited near the house as you do not want to walk too far if you should need a few herbs for the kitchen in a hurry.

An informally planted collection of herbs including lavender and mint.

USEFUL CULINARY HERBS

Chives

Chives (*Allium schoenoprasum*) are easy-to-grow perennial herbs; they have long thin leaves with an onion flavour and are excellent chopped and used in many ways in the kitchen. An attractive garnish for salads, quiches and soups. Chives make a good edging to a border, especially when they are in bloom.

Mint

Out of all the herbs that people use and grow, mint must be the favourite; even if people do not have other herbs in the garden, there is always a clump of mint. Spearmint (*Mentha spicata*) is the one that is usually grown; it has green elongated leaves and pale mauve flowers, is very invasive and the roots should be restricted otherwise they become a weed in the garden. This mint has the best flavour for making mint sauce.

If you want a mint that looks attractive as well as being tasty you should grow variegated ginger mint (*Mentha × gentilis* 'Variegata'). It has green leaves with bright yellow stripes, which remain variegated all through the summer. Not quite so vigorous in growth as other mints.

Mint likes to grow in rich, moisture-retentive soil in sun or half shade.

Sage

Sage (*Salvia officinalis*) is a small evergreen shrub that likes to grow in well-drained soil in a sunny position. In cold areas it needs some protection against frost and cold winds in the winter. Sage has grey-green felty leaves that have a strong flavour; it sometimes produces flowers which are purple. Purple sage (*Salvia officinalis* 'Purpurescens') has attractive purple leaves and makes a good background for other green-leaved herbs.

· 7 ·

Fruit

Fruit trees like apples and pears were either incorporated into the kitchen garden or grown in a mixed border with perennials and annuals, perhaps even with some rose bushes planted nearby as well. There was always a good selection of fruit trees, including many varieties of apples; some of the apples were grown especially for making into cider which was an essential part of country life.

ORCHARD FRUIT TREES

If there was plenty of ground available, fruit trees were grown in small orchards. These orchards contained a mixture of apples, pears, cherries, damsons and plums, sometimes even medlars and quinces as well.

Chickens, geese and ducks were often kept in runs and coops between the trees in an orchard. In the summer sheep were allowed to graze in the orchard and this helped to keep down the weeds.

Apples

If you live in an old cottage you might be lucky to have the remains of an orchard in your garden. Gnarled old fruit trees can add to the character of a garden by training roses, honeysuckle or clematis up the trees and it's lovely to sit in the shade of an old apple tree on a hot summer's day. Many of these old fruit trees will produce quite good crops of fruit year after year with little or no pruning. But they will not last for ever and you should plant new trees to take the place eventually of the old ones.

Many of the old fruit varieties had excellent flavour and many of these varieties are still available today. When you replant choose between the following varieties of dessert apples: 'Charles Ross', 'Ellison's Orange' and 'Worcester Pearmain'. For cooking apples choose varieties that crop well nearly every year: 'Annie Elizabeth', 'Lanes Prince Albert' and 'Rev. W. Wilks'.

Damsons and plums

If the soil was suitable, damsons, gages and plums were also grown in the old orchards. These fruit prefer to grow in alkaline soil, so if you have not got the right conditions you will have to lime the ground in the winter. Do not grow them in wet gardens or ones that are a frost pocket as the blossom appears in early spring only to be caught by the frost in such gardens.

Damsons were frequently grown in old cottage gardens where they were often planted in a field hedge on the boundary. They seemed to thrive there and did not take up so much space. However, many of the old damson trees have now disappeared, either dug up or just cut down. One should think of planting a damson tree if space is available, as damsons make one of the tastiest jams. Other stone fruit to grow include *Plum* 'Victoria' and a greengage.

61

Peaches, pears, cherries

Although peaches, pears and cherries can be grown in an orchard they are much better trained on a wall or fence. They can then get more protection from frost or winds and it is easy to put nets over them to stop the birds from eating the fruit.

SOFT FRUIT IN THE KITCHEN GARDEN

When fruit trees were grown in the kitchen garden they were planted together at one end and near a hedge or fence so as not to waste space. There were usually two or three apple trees, plus a pear, plum and damson if there was enough room. In front of the trees there were rows of soft fruit, which could be used in summer for pie and tart fillings, but was most successfully used for making jam, jelly, as well as being bottled for winter use.

Today soft fruit is still widely planted in gardens, and there are new hybrid berries to try growing. You cannot beat the flavour of freshly picked and eaten soft fruit like raspberries and strawberries. Even if you have a small garden, there is usually room for one or two fruit bushes, or you could grow strawberries in a container or special barrel.

The secret to growing soft fruit successfully is that the ground must be well fed. If you have taken over neglected soft fruit you will need to mulch the soil round the bushes with a thick layer of well-rotted manure or spent mushroom compost and the bushes will need to be pruned hard to get them into shape again. If the bushes are very old and woody it is often better to dig them up and start again with new plants. Dig the ground over deeply before replanting and if well-rotted manure is not available, bonemeal can be forked into the soil instead.

If you are starting a new soft fruit area in your garden there are a few important factors to remember. First of all the choice of site: soft fruit likes to grow in a sunny position and if possible sheltered from cold north-east winds. Don't grow soft fruit where the soil is waterlogged in winter or in a frost pocket. Most soft fruit flower early in spring and it is disappointing if it is caught by hard frosts. Second, remove all perennial weeds and dig thoroughly, incorporating plenty of manure and compost into the ground. (See under Preparation of Soil on page 52). Then you will be ready for planting which can be done at any time of the year if the plants are container grown. Bare-rooted plants can be put in the autumn before the ground is too wet or cold, or in the early spring. They are best planted in the autumn as this gives them a chance to get established before the cold weather. Remember to water them in if the weather is dry.

Blackcurrants

Blackcurrants grow best in good well-manured soil that does not dry out too much. Blackcurrants fruit on new wood and are only grown as a bush. When you have planted a new blackcurrant bush, you should prune it straight away by cutting back any stems to just one bud above the ground level. During the summer many new stems will grow and these will bear fruit the following year. Old established blackcurrant bushes can be pruned in the autumn by cutting out about a third of the old wood. But a far easier way is to cut off the branches with ripe fruit on them during the summer; this will make picking of the fruit much quicker and will also prune the bush at the same time.

Varieties: 'Wellington XXX' produces a large crop of early maturing blackcurrants with an excellent flavour; a reliable old variety. 'The

Raven' is a vigorous-growing plant which has large juicy fruits. 'Goliath' is a very old variety; it produces large-sized tasty fruits and is a good cropper every year.

Currants, red and white

Red and white currants enjoy the same soil conditions as gooseberries and also like to grow in a sunny position. They can be trained as a bush, standard, cordon or fan-shaped plant. If you have a wall or fence round your kitchen garden, these currants can be planted near them and then trained on wires fixed to the wall or fence (Fig. 13). This is an ideal way to grow them as they get protection from cold winds and it is very easy to hang nets from the wires to keep the ripening fruit away from birds. Prune these currants as you would a gooseberry (see below).

Red and white currants are not so widely grown now and it is a pity they have gone out of fashion as they will fruit well every year and are excellent for making jelly with. The raw fruit looks attractive when used in a fresh fruit salad.

Varieties: 'Laxtons No. 1' is an early-ripening red currant that produces long strings of large red fruits. 'Red Lake', the most popular of all red currants, has a large crop every year. 'White Versailles' is the best white currant to grow, and will give you delicious large fruits in early summer.

Gooseberries

Gooseberries like to grow in well-manured soil that does not dry out too much during spring and early summer. They would be planted 1.5 m (5 ft) apart and bushes trained as single cordons 45 cm (18 in) apart. Gooseberries can be trained in many ways as a bush, cordon, fan and standard. If grown as a standard the fruit is much easier to pick and there is less risk of you being scratched

Fig. 13 Ways of training soft fruit, such as raspberries, blackberries and loganberries.

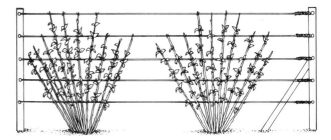

(a) Fan-trained.

(b) Blackberries or loganberries.

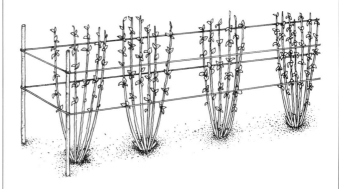

(c) Raspberries grown between two rows of wired canes 30 cm (12 in) apart.

by the prickles. Standards are simple to keep in shape once a good framework of branches has been formed. Gooseberries fruit on old wood and all you have to do in the autumn is to cut back the new growth to a bud about 8 cm (3 in) from the old wood.

You will get a few problems from mildew and sawfly caterpillars attacking the gooseberry bushes, plus damage caused by birds pecking out the fruit buds.

Give your gooseberry bushes plenty of water in dry weather once the fruit has begun to form, otherwise you will not get large juicy fruits.

Varieties: 'Leveller' crops well every year and has large fruit which can be eaten raw when they have turned yellow and are properly ripe. 'Whinham Industry' is another reliable cropper which produces large red gooseberries; this variety will tolerate some shade. 'Careless' has a good-flavoured fruit, again crops well every year and will grow well in most types of soil. 'Invicta' is a mildew-resistant variety bearing a good crop of large fruits.

Raspberries

Raspberries are surely one of the most delicious of all summer soft fruits and they should be eaten as soon as possible after picking to get the full flavour of the fruit. Even in a small garden there should be room for a few raspberry canes. Where space is limited they can be grown in a narrow border in front of a fence, using canes tied to wires.

Raspberries require rich, well-manured ground that is moisture retentive. They need plenty of water in early summer in order to produce large juicy fruits.

Varieties: 'Malling Delight' has very large fruit and crops very well every year. 'Malling Admiral' produces large fruits with excellent flavour, and is one of the best varieties for freezing.

◀ Gooseberries are a traditional cottage garden soft fruit which have many uses in the kitchen.

▶ Blackcurrants and raspberries are among the most delicious of all summer fruit and should be eaten as soon as possible after picking.

· 8 ·
Incorporating Features

Old country cottages and their gardens abound with interesting features, all of which were included for a specific purpose. Gates and fences were built to keep cattle and sheep out of the garden. Paths of brick and stone led from the gate to the front door or side door. Porches and trellis-work surrounded the doorways, to help stop the wind and rain from coming in through cracks or gaps round the door (old cottages were often very damp and draughty inside). There was always a nearby well and various outhouses, even an old privy and perhaps a pig sty. Today these features can be incorporated into a modern cottage garden, although some may need restoration work.

ARTIFICIAL BOUNDARIES

Walls

Walls come in many sizes and can be made from brick, stone or flints. They are strong and will help to keep some animals out of your garden, although squirrels and cats will just climb over. Walls will stop some wind and, if they are south-west facing, will give plants protection against frosts.

Mellow brick or stone walls make an excellent background for flowering plants (Fig. 14). By creating a border in front of a wall you will highlight this feature. If the wall is tall you can train climbing plants up it with perennials or annuals in front. When the wall is made of brick you will need to grow plants that have brightly coloured flowers and foliage, otherwise they will not show up against a dark background. Some walls were built of flint and others were of dry stone, and their cracks and crevices were used to grow plants. On the north-facing side ferns, lichen and mosses thrived while on the sunny side aubrieta, houseleeks and valerian grew in every available cracks.

Old walls look wonderful but one disadvantage is that many snails will live and hibernate in all the crevices.

Fences (Fig. 15)

● *Wooden* Most fences were and are still made of wood which does not last as long as a wall, but is easy to replace. Today many types of wooden fencing can be used, including chestnut paling, rail and post, lattice and picket. The lattice fence is made from rustic poles or wood arranged in criss-cross pattern – a short fence suitable for a boundary. The picket fence, which is ideal for enclosing the front garden of a cottage, is made by nailing slats of wood on horizontal rails. It is not a solid fence as the slats are spaced 5 cm (2 in) apart. Gates can be made to match the fence.

Some people like to paint their fences, green or white being the most common colours. Rambling roses or clematis can be woven between the slats,

Fig. 14 **Some of the different types of walls that can be used in a cottage garden.**

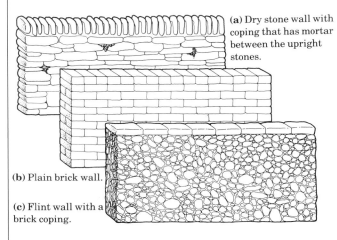

(a) Dry stone wall with coping that has mortar between the upright stones.

(b) Plain brick wall.

(c) Flint wall with a brick coping.

Fig. 15 **Different types of fencing which can be used as a boundary or for dividing parts of a garden.**

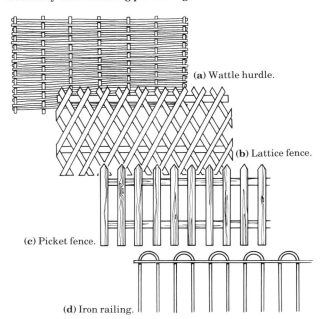

(a) Wattle hurdle.

(b) Lattice fence.

(c) Picket fence.

(d) Iron railing.

while lupins, poppies and other perennials in the beds in front of the fence will all add to the overall cottage-garden look.

● *Wattle hurdles* that are made from hazel poles and sticks are good if you need a quickly erected fence. Each hurdle has a strong pointed stake at either end which is just pushed into the ground. They make wonderful wind breaks and are good for keeping animals out of a garden. If you live in an exposed position and want to plant an evergreen hedge or shrubbery, hurdles can be used to give protection to the young plants. Position the hurdles about 60 cm (24 in) away from the plants.

● *Iron railings* were once used for fencing and you will still see some examples today. Many have remained in good condition and just need a coat of paint every few years.

GATES AND GATEWAYS

Gates and gateways should look inviting and in keeping with the nearby walls, fences or hedges. Very ornamental wrought-iron gates will look out of place in a cottage garden where a wooden one will be more suitable.

If you have a wide drive, a wooden farm gate is a practical choice; they are very hard-wearing and will last for many years given a yearly coat of boiled linseed oil. For gardens that have a hedge round them, a wooden farm gate is most appropriate.

Wicket gates
A wicket gate is a typical country cottage feature, useful as well as decorative. These gates are made from wooden slates and are often painted green, blue or white. Ideally suited as an entrance between hedges or picket fences. A rustic trellis over the gateway, with climbing plants trained

67

◄ This attractive wall and wooden gate invites you to walk up the path to the cottage beyond.

► Old walls, wooden gates and stone paving create interesting features in a cottage garden.

over it, will add to the character of the entrance, making it inviting to walk through and see what is on the other side.

Iron gates

Iron gates will last a lifetime if they are properly looked after and not allowed to go rusty. A regular painting programme is needed to keep them in good condition. If you have a wall enclosing your garden, you will find that an iron gate is very suitable to use as an entrance. Where walls have a tall pillar either side of a gateway, an iron archway is sometimes used to bridge that gap. The plain archway is best, with roses and honeysuckle climbing and twining round the ironwork, to fill the air with fragrance on a warm sunny day in summer.

PATHS

So many different types of materials were used to make a path, from gravel, stone chippings, bricks, paving slabs to even solid concrete ones. Old cottage paths were always put down for a purpose, which we tend easily to forget today. A cottager would make a path from his gate to the front door; another would lead to the back or side door, with a straight one leading from there to the end of the garden. Nowadays we like our paths to look ornamental as well as to be useful, so they are more likely to be curved as a change from the straight lines. We now also have many more kinds of stone slabs and bricks to choose from, which makes laying a path more simple than it used to be.

69

Always make a plan first before laying a new path, then mark out the area with pegs, taking care to get the levels right before you begin.

Brick paths

What a wonderful feature a traditional brick path creates in a cottage garden, especially when the path is bordered by flower beds and the plants are allowed to tumble over the edge of the path. Although old bricks look more mellow, they will sometimes crumble after frosty weather and over many years of constant use will wear away. There are new bricks available that are dark brick red with black mottled markings on them to make them look old; these bricks are very hard-wearing.

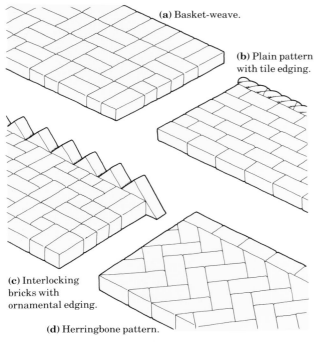

(a) Basket-weave.

(b) Plain pattern with tile edging.

(c) Interlocking bricks with ornamental edging.

(d) Herringbone pattern.

Fig. 16 Designs for brick paths. There are many ways of laying bricks for attractive paths.

The bricks in paths may be laid in straight lines or curved and in a variety of patterns, including herringbone which looks most attractive of all. Other interesting patterns include the basket-weave (Fig. 16).

Stone slabs

Cottages and their many features were always built in whatever material that was available near at hand, as obviously it was too difficult and costly to transport stone, bricks or flint far. If you are lucky to live in an area where stone is readily available, it is very likely that stone was used for making paths as well as a house or cottage.

Old stone paths are extremely hard-wearing and make a good foil for nearby plants. Wide borders either side of a stone path should be filled with perennials and annuals that have blue or pink flowers. These colours look marvellous when complementing grey mellow stone.

Paving slabs

Paving slabs are good for making a wide solid path through a vegetable garden, where one is likely to be pushing a well-laden wheelbarrow. It is much easier to push a wheelbarrow full of manure along a proper path than to try to push it along an uneven one. Make sure when laying a new path that the slabs are all level.

Crazy paving

Many of the old cottages had paths made of crazy paving as this was a lot cheaper than buying in whole paving slabs. Crazy paving is just slabs that have got broken. These paths look very effective but it is a slow painstaking job to make one and you would be advised to get professional help. Sand or a nearly dry mortar can be brushed between the pieces to make a stable path. Leave one or two holes in the path in which to grow small low-growing plants. Thymes are ideal for this purpose as when they are trodden on, they emit a wonderful fragrance.

Gravel paths

A gravel path will give you that informal cottage-garden look, especially if plants are allowed to sprawl over the edge of the path. Herbaceous borders with penstemons, pinks, aquilegias, hardy geraniums and grey foliage plants either side of a gravel path look particularly effective.

Gravel paths are very easy to construct but you must put up retaining boards before tipping in the gravel. Gravel is constantly on the move and unless there is an edge to stop it, will spread out into a flower bed. Problems are often caused when the path has a lawn on either side, as gravel thrown up on the lawn will spoil the blades of the mower.

PORCHES AND TRELLIS

Many cottages have some kind of porch or trellis round their front door and these form an important feature. In particular, porches are essential if the cottage is thatched, as people do not want to get soaked by drips pouring off the thatch on a rainy day when standing by the door talking to someone inside. They can be a very simple structure or more ornate.

Thatched cottages have thatched porches which can be supported by two strong posts sited either side of the door. They are very simple and easy to erect. If a more waterproof porch is needed, the sides can be bricked up or wood can be used. Windows can be put in the sides to let in more light.

A large porch can have a bench seat built into the structure on both sides. You will find it is very restful to sit in a sheltered porch watching the world go by. It's even better if climbing plants grown for their fragrance are trained over the porch. Climbing or rambling roses, honeysuckle and jasmine can be planted for this purpose, together with sweet peas.

· CLIMBING SHRUBS ·	
Name	**Description**
Akebia quinata	Semi-evergreen twining plant with maroon fragrant flowers
Chinese wisteria (Wisteria sinensis)	Long racemes of mauve fragrant flowers
Clematis	
● fern-leaved (Clematis cirrhosa balearica)	Evergreen clematis with pale yellow flowers during winter
● 'Nellie Moser'	Pale pink flowers with a broad rose pink stripe
● orange peel (Clematis orientalis)	Yellow flowers with sepals that look like orange peel
Climbing hydrangea (Hydrangea petiolaris)	Self-supporting climber with lace-cap type flowers
Common white jasmine (Jasminum officinalis)	Clusters of tiny, sweetly scented white flowers
Honeysuckle	
● Japanese (Lonicera japonica aureoreticulata)	Small fragrant flowers with variegated leaves
● Late Dutch (Lonicera periclymenum)	Red buds followed by cream flowers
Ivy (Hedera colchica 'Sulphur Heart')	Large green leaves with yellow markings
Passion flower (Passiflora caerulea)	Large flowers that are green-white, slightly scented
Rose	
● R. 'Goldfinch'	Sprays of small yellow flowers that fade to white
● R. 'Zephirine Drouhin'	A bright pink, sweetly scented climbing rose.
Trumpet vine (Campsis radicans)	Bright orange red trumpet flowers in summer
Virginia creeper (Parthenocissus quinquefolia)	The best creeper for autumn colour when the leaves turn scarlet

In winter half-hardy perennials that have been grown in pots can be stood under the porch to give them some protection from rain and slight frosts. However, in extreme cold and frosty weather, it is important that these half-hardy plants should be taken inside.

Trellis-work

Trellises can be fixed to a wall and used as a framework for climbing and twining plants to grow through. They can also be used to create an archway or to give extra height on top of a wall or fence. Trellises were made of wood slats nailed together to form interesting patterns and shapes; others were made from rustic poles. Now you can buy trellis that is made from plastic. It may last longer but does not look so good.

You can buy panels of trellis at garden centres and they are easy to erect. There is a great choice of size and pattern, the two most popular ones being the diamond-shaped lattice pattern and the one with small squares of slatted wood.

OUTHOUSES AND SHEDS

Old cottage gardens contained a large number of extra buildings and sheds. These were built for many reasons, often giving the cottager extra room for storing, washing, baking, plus places that were used for housing animals. Outhouses and sheds were made of brick, stone, wood, flint and corrugated iron. If you are lucky enough to have any of these buildings in your garden, they can be made to feature prominently.

Bake-houses and wash-houses

A bake-house or wash-house was a small separate building close to the cottage which was used for baking and also to do the washing in. There was a range with an oven where cooking was done and a large copper for heating the water that was used for the washing. These coppers were built into a brick surround and the water heated by a fire that was lit underneath it. As these buildings were warm and dry they made an excellent store-room.

Nowadays this type of outhouse is sometimes converted into a garage, but it is much better to use it as storage space. Ideal for tools, garden machinery, garden furniture and storing onions, shallots, even potatoes, as long as it is not kept too warm (it just needs to be frost free). If the walls are made of brick, flint or stone they will provide a good background for climbing or wall plants, which will create an interesting feature in your garden.

An old privy, which was usually sited away from the cottage, can be converted into a store or even a small summer house. It is surprising how many ways old outhouses can be used.

◄ How well this little wooden gate blends in with the surrounding flower borders containing alliums and *Alchemilla mollis*.

A wooden water butt makes an interesting feature in a cottage garden, as well as being useful for collecting rainwater.

Converting pig sties

Pig sties can be made into a place for storing logs, and if it has a flint or stone wall enclosing it, you could convert the area into a tiny courtyard garden. It would be quite simple to make some raised beds against the walls in which to grow herbs or alpines, but they would need a sunny position. If it was shady you could grow plants like ferns and hostas. If the pig sty has a corrugated iron roof it will need to be camouflaged. An evergreen climbing plant like a variegated ivy is very suitable.

73

Sheds

Nearly every cottage had a shed in the garden, which was filled with a marvellous assortment of tools, fertilizers, string, canes, old packets of seeds and odd pieces of wire. The tools were always kept in a very neat and tidy way, each having its own place in the shed, either on a shelf or hanging from a nail. The tools were cleaned and then wiped with an oily rag before being put away.

Today, with many of the tools being made of stainless steel, it is easier to keep them in good condition, but they should be put away in the right place after you have finished using them. Tools, especially secateurs and trowels, are soon lost if left out in the garden. There is still a need to have a shed for tools and garden machinery, although some people have large garages where they can keep their tools. Wooden sheds can be tucked into a corner of the garden, or made into a feature by having paving in front of the shed. This can be used for growing plants in pots or as a nursery area for young plants being raised.

OTHER FEATURES

Wells

It must be remembered that it was difficult and hard work to keep all the vegetables, fruit and flowers watered in old cottage gardens before mains water was available. To keep plants growing happily in dry weather a cottager would have to water the garden by using a watering can, a long painstaking job without the convenience of a hose. The water would be carried from a pond, stream or brought up from a well. Some wells had a pump attached which made drawing water quicker. Many of the old cottages had their own well, but the water would sometimes be shared with other nearby cottages. Wells, or more so the

wellheads, are a super cottage garden feature and can be made one of the focal points of a cottage garden.

I am lucky to have a real well just outside the front door of my cottage and have created an interesting feature for that part of the garden by positioning pots near the well. The well has a brick surround with an ornamental wrought-iron wellhead, over which climbers are trained. The pots stand on a brick and flint path that circles the well.

Many wellheads were made from wood with an attachment for winding up the water; this type of well is most people's idea of an old cottage well.

It is most important to remember that wells can be a potentially dangerous hazard in a garden, especially if there are small children about. Everyone likes to look down wells and to drop coins down them to see how deep they are. It is easy for a child to slip and fall down a well and it can be very difficult to pull someone out. Always have a heavy cover over the mouth of the well, then stand a large pot of container on top of it, so that the lid cannot be moved in a hurry.

During the past few years many people have decided to restore their wells into working condition, in order to use the water for their gardens. In drought summers, it is helpful to have your own water supply.

Pumps

The old cast-iron pumps look very attractive in a garden; some were of a simple design while others were very ornate. They can easily be restored and used for pumping water from a well, and they work very efficiently with little maintenance.

To create an eye-catching feature near a pump, try to find an old stone trough or sink to place under the pump to catch the drips. The trough will soon be covered in lichen and mosses, even ferns. When this happens it is good for wildlife as bees and sometimes butterflies will alight on damp moss to suck up the moisture in hot weather.

A grouping of different sizes of planted-up pots and containers near the pump will add to this typical country-cottage feature.

Reproduction cast-iron pumps can now be purchased but they need to mellow before they will have the same character and look as effective as an old pump.

Water butts

As there was always a need to conserve water for the summer months, water butts and storage tanks were widely used. These water butts were positioned under drainpipes and gutters to collect rainwater that fell on the roof. There was always at least one large water butt or barrel in every cottage garden. Nowadays we have only started to realize again the importance of saving water in this way. Most of our surface water goes down a drain and does not benefit the garden at all.

Wooden water butts or barrels look best in a cottage garden but always keep some water in the bottom. If they do dry out completely the wood will shrink and leaks will occur when they are next filled with rain. In very hot dry weather layers of damp sacking can be put round the butts to stop them drying out.

Wooden seats and benches

A garden should not be a place just for working in, it should also be enjoyed as a place for relaxing in. Have one or two seats or benches in different parts of your garden; site one in a sunny sheltered spot and another in a shady position (Fig. 17).

Wooden seats and benches are more in keeping with a cottage garden. A simple country bench can be made by putting a plank on top of two logs.

Cold frames

If you do not have a greenhouse, it is useful to have a cold frame in which to start off seedlings in the spring. You could site a frame in the same area as the shed or have one or two in the kitchen garden.

Frames were more widely used in old cottage gardens than they are now. These frames were sometimes half filled with well-rotted manure to create a hot bed; they would be planted with marrows, ridge cucumbers and even melons in the spring to produce an early crop. This method is worth trying even today.

These old types of frames were a permanent structure made of brick or wood with a glass top, a good thing to have in a garden. New frames are more versatile in that they are nearly always made of all glass and can be moved if required. But most people now use cloches instead of frames.

Fig. 17 Two designs of rustic seats which are very easy to make.

(a) Bench made from a plank of wood nailed down on the top of two round logs.

(b) Seat sewn out of a piece of log, easily cut with a chain saw.

·9·
Using Containers

Good use of containers will create extra colourful features in a cottage garden, but you do need to choose the right type of container that will not look out of place in this kind of setting. Use traditional clay or terracotta pots and planters if possible and not the plain plastic ones.

As cottagers hated to throw things away, they would adapt all manner of containers in which to grow their plants in. Tubs, barrels, old milk churns, pieces of drainpipe, old cast iron saucepans and wooden wheelbarrows could all be filled with compost and planted up.

There are endless possibilities of where to position your containers; by the front door is one of the most favoured sites. Most people change the plants in their containers twice a year. Grow annuals and half-hardy perennials for summer colour. Later, after these have been removed, in the autumn the containers can be planted with winter and spring-flowering bulbs, plus biennials like wallflowers, forget-me-nots and winter-flowering pansies.

POSITIONING THE CONTAINERS

By doorways
Either side of a door is ideal as they make the entrance look more attractive. Grow fragrant flowers in some of the containers so you will get the full benefit of the lovely scents when going in or out of the door.

If you are planting up containers for winter and spring colour, stand them near a doorway or under a window. Then you will be able to see the lovely spring-flowering bulbs without having to go into the garden on very wet or cold days.

On steps and terraces
Many gardens have steps or terraces and these make an attractive background on which to place pots, tubs or troughs. Trailing plants are very suitable for these positions as they will tumble over the steps as well as the containers. Do not grow plants that have thorns or prickles too close to steps or stairs as people would not like to be scratched when walking past. Do not grow plants that break easily when knocked on steps. The plants need to be tough in order to withstand people rushing past.

On paved areas
Old stone troughs look wonderful when positioned on a paved area. These troughs filled with alpines and dwarf spring-flowering bulbs will make a good feature in areas which have been paved with brick or mellow stone. There are often paved areas near outhouses or pig sties, all useful

▶ **The good use of old chimney pots creates a charming feature for a cottage garden.**

places for positioning pots and tubs, especially when there is a wall behind. Climbers can then be planted in the containers to train up the walls.

There is an important point to remember if you stand containers on any type of paving: that is, the base of the container will often freeze to the paving in frosty weather which could cause clay or terracotta pots to crack. To avoid this, stand them on short legs or raise them slightly off the ground.

By wells and pumps

In order to make wells and pumps more of a feature in a cottage garden, place containers of different shapes and sizes nearby. Pots, old buckets and barrels all look right near a well, as containers should blend in with the surroundings.

Old watering cans and even galvanized buckets make suitable containers for putting next to a pump.

TYPES OF CONTAINERS

The choice of suitable containers for cottage gardens is endless and they need not be expensive. Look round second-hand shops and where old houses are being knocked down; you will be surprised just how many kinds of unusual containers you will find.

Clay and terracotta pots (Fig. 18)

In many ways traditional clay pots look more in keeping with cottage gardens than any other type of container. Traditional clay pots are readily available in many sizes from very small to giant-sized ones. Almost all plants will grow well in a clay pot, but they do dry out much quicker than plastic ones and have to be watered more often.

Clay pots are best for alpines that need free-draining soil and also for half-hardy perennials

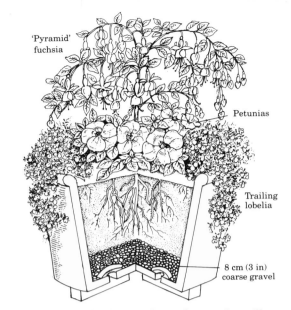

'Pyramid' fuchsia

Petunias

Trailing lobelia

8 cm (3 in) coarse gravel

Fig. 18 Ideas for planting up a large clay pot that will provide non-stop summer flowering.

like yellow marguerite (*Argyranthemum frutescens* 'Jamaica Primrose') and heliotrope or cherry pie (*Heliotropium* 'Chatsworth'). Herbs are also plants that grow well in clay or terracotta pots, as many herbs come from Mediterranean countries with dry sunny climates.

People worry about clay or terracotta pots being frost proof and this is indeed a problem. Some makes of clay pots are guaranteed frost proof but others will crack in very frosty weather. This can be avoided to some extent, especially when planting up large pots, if you put an 8 cm (3 in) layer of very coarse gravel in the bottom of the pot, then fill with soil or compost. The pot is less likely to get so waterlogged in winter or to freeze solid in cold weather. If the soil is very wet when it freezes, it will expand, which sometimes cracks the pot.

In extreme cold weather move pots to a more sheltered position or wrap plastic round the pot for extra protection (sacking or even bracken can be used for this purpose). Some pots are glazed on the outside and this will help to protect them against frost. Other pots may be decorated (the larger pots look very attractive when decorated).

Clay and terracotta is used not only for pots, but for large bowls, small troughs and special planters as well. The large bowls are excellent for planting bulbs, alpines or herbs in.

Wooden containers

Wooden tubs, whole or half barrels and buckets are typical cottage-garden containers. Cottagers would use these types of containers for putting plants in when they were no longer any good for holding liquids. Barrels and tubs that leaked were still good for holding soil.

Large wooden tubs and barrels are ideal containers for permanent planting. Many kinds of shrubs are suitable for growing in containers. They include skimmias, dwarf hebes, witch hazels, hydrangeas and roses. By filling the containers with ericaceous compost, they can be planted with acid-loving shrubs like camellias and azaleas.

Climbers such as clematis, honeysuckle and passion flowers will grow happily in large tubs and barrels that have a good depth of soil, as they need plenty of space for their roots in order to grow well.

Annuals, pelargoniums, fuchsias and bulbs are also suitable for growing in wooden containers. Holes may be drilled in the side of the barrel and then filled with bulbs or trailing annuals.

Another use for a barrel is to plant it up with strawberries (Fig. 19); this will look very attractive when the strawberries are ripe. Once the strawberries have begun to flower, do not let the soil dry out completely and keep the barrel well watered in order to produce juicy fruit.

Make sure that new barrels, tubs and buckets have drainage holes in the bottom before filling with compost. Then put a layer of gravel or

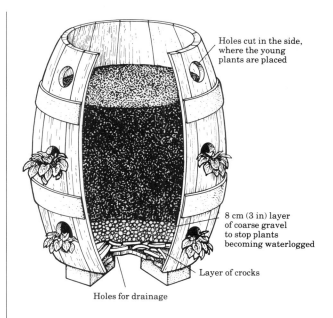

Holes cut in the side, where the young plants are placed

8 cm (3 in) layer of coarse gravel to stop plants becoming waterlogged

Layer of crocks

Holes for drainage

Fig. 19 Strawberries can be grown most successfully in a large barrel.

broken crocks in the bottom to ensure that the container will not get waterlogged in very wet weather, add the compost on top and firm down. Do not fill containers right to the very top as you must leave room to be able to water the plants properly.

Wheelbarrows

Wooden and galvanized wheelbarrows can both be used as interesting planters. Once planted up they will give very colourful displays as they give a good depth of soil and you will be able to get many plants in a limited area.

Remember to check that there are good drainage holes in the wheelbarrow before you fill and plant it up. Wheelbarrows can be used for permanent plants or seasonal ones.

Unusual containers

There are numerous unusual containers which can be successfully adapted for growing plants in.

● *Old cast-iron saucepans, kettles and cauldrons* It does not matter if they have some holes in the bottom, as this will save you having to make some. If the bottom has nearly rusted away, it can be strengthened by lining it with a metal sheet with holes in it. If the hole outside is rusty this can be brushed off with a wire brush, then painted with a suitable primer before applying the top coat; black or grey looks best.

● *Chimney pots and lengths of drain-pipe* will make interesting containers, especially if they are made of clay. Chimney pots are good for

These daffodils look lovely planted in this unusual stone basket-like pot.

shrubs or climbers as they will give you a good depth of soil. Small pieces of drain-pipe are excellent for alpines like sempervivums that need good drainage.

● *Old milk churns* can be adapted into useful containers, although they will need holes made in the bottom before planting up. They should have about 15 cm (6 in) of rubble or coarse gravel in the bottom to give plenty of drainage. Unless the churn has ample drainage the soil will get waterlogged. Churns can be left a natural metal colour or painted. Some people paint very ornate patterns on them, which look very attractive in the right setting.

PLANTS FOR CONTAINERS

Bulbs for spring colour (Fig. 20)

Bulbs will provide very colourful displays in spring as they are easy to grow and are ideally suited for containers of any shape or size. The dwarf flowering bulbs are good for window boxes, troughs and small pots.

Crocuses can be planted in small pots or round the edge of larger containers; plant in groups of three or five to give maximum effect. The following varieties will grow well in containers: *Crocus* 'Snowbunting', which has lovely white flowers with orange stamens'; *C.* 'Zwanenburg Bronze', an unusual-coloured crocus with yellow petals that have broad deep maroon stripes on the backs of the petals; and *C.* 'Ruby Giant' which has mauvish-blue flowers. All flower in early spring.

Plant groups of *Anemone blanda*, chionodoxas and puschkinias between the crocuses.

Irises, the bulbous early spring-flowering varieties, will grow happily in clay pots, shallow stone troughs and sinks. They are a delightful flower that needs to grow in a sunny position in well-drained soil. There are several different species and varieties to choose from: *I. reticulata* 'Cantab', lovely pale blue flowers with orange markings; and *I. reticulata* 'Pauline', which is a pale lilac blue iris with darker veining and markings.

Dwarf tulips are suitable for planting in clay or terracotta pots and in other containers with free-draining soil in a sunny position. Many will start to bloom in early spring, but the flowering time will depend on the weather.

There are many charming little species of tulips, including *Tulipa pulchella* 'Violacea' which has mauvy red blooms, very dwarf in habit; *T. turkestanica*, a multi-headed pale yellow tulip with a darker centre; and *T. urumiensis* with yellow flowers and multi-headed, growing to 10 cm (4 in) tall.

For large containers try the following: *T.* 'Couleur Cardinal' with plum-coloured blooms and a dark stem 30 cm (12 in) tall; *T.* 'Apricot Beauty', a lovely soft apricot tulip; and *T.* 'West Point', an unusual bright yellow lily-flowered tulip which has pointed petals 56 cm (22 in) tall and flowers in late spring or early summer. The taller tulips look best when planted with wallflowers, forget-me-nots and winter-flowering pansies. These can be of contrasting colours or shades to match the colour of the tulips.

Daffodils Out of all the varieties of dwarf daffodils *Narcissus* 'Tête-à-Tête' must be the most reliable and widely planted one for use in containers. It has bright yellow petals with a slightly orange-yellow trumpet, a multi-headed daffodil. *N.* 'Hawera' is a beautiful pale yellow, small-flowered narcissus; it has several blooms on each stem and the leaves are thin and grass-like. *N.* 'Minnow' has several small flowers per stem; they have white petals and tiny yellow trumpets and look lovely when planted in stone sinks and troughs.

Wooden tubs are a traditional container to use in a cottage garden, this one planted for summer colour with pansies and marguerites.

The taller-growing daffodils are superb for all types of medium to large containers. If there is a good depth of soil the bulbs can be planted in two layers. This will give you a wonderful display of colour in spring. *N.* 'St Keverne' has bright yellow flowers that will last for many weeks; a very reliable, large-cupped daffodil that starts to bloom in early spring and grows to 45 cm (18 in) tall.

Hyacinths are the most colourful of all spring-flowering bulbs. Closely planted in containers, these bulbs will create eye-catching displays for

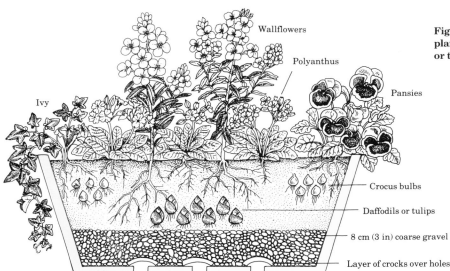

Wallflowers

Polyanthus

Pansies

Ivy

Crocus bulbs

Daffodils or tulips

8 cm (3 in) coarse gravel

Layer of crocks over holes

Fig. 20 Suggestions for planting up a large container or tub for spring colour.

many weeks. Containers are best planted with hyacinths of all the same colour as other colours do not always bloom at the same time. The following varieties all do well planted in outdoor containers; *H.* 'Blue Magic' has deep blue flowers with a white eye; *H.* 'Distinction' has flowers of an unusual shape of deep plum red, quite different from the normal colours of hyacinths; and *H.* 'L' Innocence' has pure white flowers.

Summer-flowering annuals

Half-hardy annuals are the most widely used plants for creating stunning summer displays and there is a vast range to choose from. They can be planted in any sort of container both large and small. Most popular are petunias, trailing lobelia, impatiens, nemesia and alyssum. All can be grown easily from seed, started under glass in spring or bought as young plants ready to put into your containers in early summer.

Petunias will flower throughout the summer and early autumn, ideal for all medium and large containers. They need to grow in fairly free-

draining soil and in a sunny position; they will not grow at all well in a shady place. They look lovely in clay pots or a wooden wheelbarrow when closely planted together with an edging of trailing lobelia.

Petunias come in shades of mauve, blue, red, pink and some varieties are more resistant to damp and wet weather. They are easily grown from seed, or young plants are available from nurseries and garden centres. Good varieties to grow from seed include *P.* 'Celebrity Applause' which has flowers in shades of lilac, blue and white, some with darker veining on the petals. If you like double flowers you can try *P.* 'Delight Mixed', which will give you a selection of double petunias in many colours, including red, pink, mauve and also bi-coloured.

Trailing lobelias are essential plants for containers as they flower throughout the summer and autumn without stopping. They are wonderful for trailing gracefully down over the edges of containers as one does not want to see too much of the pot or barrel.

Varieties to grow from seed include *Lobelia* 'Crimson Cascade', with deep red flowers; *L.* 'Lilac Fountain', with lilac pink flowers; and *L.* 'Cascade Blue', which has blue flowers, is vigorous in growth and good for trailing over large containers.

Impatiens, or busy lizzies, are very important plants for all types of containers as they are happy to grow in shade, although they will also grow in a sunny position. They will tolerate wet and dull weather more than many other bedding plants. Impatiens are really half-hardy perennials but are mainly grown as annuals.

Varieties to grow from seed include *Impatiens* 'Symphony Red Star', which has brilliant red flowers with a white centre; *I.* 'Tempo Apricot', which has flowers in apricot shades with a small white eye; or you can grow *I.* 'Tempo Jazz' mixed, which includes an amazing range of vibrant colours.

Half-hardy perennials for summer flowering

Many of the half-hardy perennials make super pot plants for summer flowering. Geraniums (pelargoniums) and marguerites (argyranthemums) are two of the favourites for this use.

Ivy-leafed geraniums look lovely in clay or terracotta pots, or wooden tubs where they will tumble over the sides. *Pelargonium peltatum* 'L'Elégante' is an old variety of ivy-leafed geranium which has pale lilac flowers with some darker veining on the petals; it is very reliable. Nowadays there are many new free-flowering varieties available, many of which have attractive variegated leaves. One of the best of the newer varieties is the charming *P. peltatum* 'Mini Cascade', a compact plant with bright red flowers which needs to be dead-headed regularly.

Marguerites (argyranthemums) are half-hardy perennials and are ideal for growing in large pots,

tubs and barrels as they make a lot of root and therefore require a good depth of soil. They like to grow in a sunny position and if possible sheltered from strong winds. They flower non-stop during summer and into autumn, stopping only when cut back by frost. If you live in a sheltered place or perhaps near the sea, marguerites can be left outside during the winter.

Argyranthemum frutescens 'Jamaica Primrose' has single yellow daisy-type flowers, is extremely free-flowering and one of the most popular; *A. frutescens* 'Vancover' is a double pink-flowered variety that looks lovely in stone containers.

Many other perennials, shrubs and climbers can also be used successfully in containers.

Fragrant plants

Always have some container-grown fragrant plants positioned near a door or window.

Sweet peas (*Lathyrus odoratus*) should be included, either the climbing ones or *L. odoratus* 'Fantasia', a dwarf, slightly trailing sweet pea very suitable for containers. These are easily grown from seed which may then be sown straight into a container.

Heliotrope or cherry pie (*Heliotropium* 'Chatsworth') is a fragrant half-hardy shrub which used to be grown more often than it is now. It has heads of tiny mauve flowers blooming for many weeks during summer.

· 10 ·
Care and Maintenance

To get the most from your cottage garden you need to adopt a regular programme of planting, feeding and maintenance, together with picking and gathering fruit and vegetables.

To simplify the list of seasonal work needed to keep a garden in good condition, this chapter is been divided into the four seasons, each with paragraphs on flowers, fruit and vegetables.

SPRING

Flowers
The arrival of spring is heralded by daffodils, crocuses, primroses and wallflowers bursting into flower. They need little maintenance apart from dead-heading the daffodils and wallflowers.

Sow primula seed under glass including polyanthus and primrose seed. Other hardy perennial seed that now can also be sown under glass includes lupins, delphiniums, polemonium and lychnis. After they have germinated and been pricked out into boxes, keep inside until the seedlings are established. Put outside in a sheltered position if the weather is suitable; do not put outside in very cold weather.

Half-hardy annuals can be sown in heated greenhouses, including petunias, trailing lobelia, asters and French marigolds. Prick out in boxes as soon as the seedlings are large enough to handle. These plants cannot be put outside until the risk of frosts has passed, usually in late spring.

Hardy annual seed can be sown direct into the soil in late spring; the seed can be sown in lines or in patches. Thin out the seedlings when necessary. Once these annuals have started to grow, place hazel twigs between them to give the plants support when they mature. Many hardy annuals, like Shirley poppies, larkspur, godetia and cornflowers, will flop over in wet or windy weather without some kind of support.

Plant gladioli corms and dahlia tubers in late spring in a sunny position. Do not plant gladioli in waterlogged soil or they will rot off. If you have moisture-retentive soil, put a thick layer of coarse gravel under the corm to give it more drainage.

Feed herbaceous borders with bonemeal or blood, or fish and bonemeal if they did not get a mulch of manure or spent mushroom compost in the autumn.

Vegetables
Spring is a very busy time in the vegetable garden. It starts in early spring with the planting of shallots and onion sets, but not when the ground is frozen. Ground that was dug over during the winter is easily raked over, then planting can begin. Shallots and onion sets are pressed into the soil to just past halfway over the bulb.

First sowing of broad beans and peas can be made now with a succession of later sowings at fortnightly intervals.

► A colourful display of spring flowers provided by tulips and polyanthus.

▼ Seeds of perennials and half-hardy annuals can be sown in early spring under glass.

Sow early-maturing varieties of lettuce under cloches; these will be ready for picking in early summer.

Sow early varieties of cauliflower and calabrese under cloches; the young plants can be moved to open ground when the risk of hard frosts have passed.

Plant first early potatoes like 'Maris Bard' and 'Vanessa'. Remember to keep earthing up the potatoes as frost will soon damage the foliage.

In late spring plant maincrop potatoes, including 'Desirée' and 'Maris Piper'.

Sow carrots, parsnips, beetroot and parsley in late spring. They are best thickly sown then thinned, as it seems to help give a good germination.

Watch out for damage caused by slugs and snails at this time of the year. They will sometimes eat parts of newly planted shallots and onion sets, also young vegetable seedlings. Use slug pellets or slug traps to catch them.

85

Fruit

It is not too late to put a thick mulch of well-rotted manure or spent mushroom compost around soft fruit bushes. If this is not available, give the fruit some blood, fish and bonemeal.

Straw or black polythene should be put around strawberries to stop fruits becoming muddy and gritty when they ripen in early summer. To get an early crop, put cloches over a few of the plants in early spring. Strawberry flowers are susceptible to frost damage in late spring; if frost warnings are given, cover plants with fibre fleece. This light material will give them protection against this type of damage.

Plants in containers

Remember to check that plants grown in containers do not dry out, as it's easy to forget to water them in spring. They can quickly dry out, especially of you grow tulips in containers, as their wide leaves hang over the container and when it rains the water tends to run over the side.

Remember to keep dead-heading pansies grown in containers to extend their flowering.

When bulbs grown in pots have finished blooming, they can be planted between perennials in a border.

SUMMER

Flowers

There are many jobs to do in the herbaceous border in early summer when they need plenty of care and attention. If you find you have a few gaps in the border, these can be filled with new perennials, or annuals can be planted in the spaces. Perhaps you could put in some new plants to attract bees and butterflies to the garden. Always remember to water the plants in well if there is dry weather.

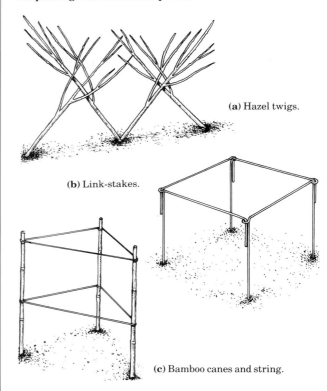

Fig. 21 **Ways of staking. Always position the stakes before the plants get too tall and flop over.**

(a) Hazel twigs.

(b) Link-stakes.

(c) Bamboo canes and string.

Go through the borders about every two weeks during the summer, removing any weeds and dead-heading at the same time. If the borders are set in a lawn, trim the edges of the lawn; this makes all the difference to the look of the garden.

● *Perennials* grow very quickly in early summer and will require staking (Fig. 21). There are many ways of doing this. Hazel twigs, metal link stakes and bamboo canes can all be used. Always be careful when using canes, especially old ones, as they get very brittle and will break when you are pushing them into the soil. Split canes can be razor sharp and can cut your hand. Be careful when you bend down in the border that tall canes do not poke you in the eye: putting plastic cups over canes will stop this happening.

● *Annuals and biennials* Plant out half-hardy bedding plants and water them in well. Sweet peas will need good sticks to support them and once they have stared to bloom they should be picked regularly to ensure continuous flowering during the summer months.

Wallflowers, forget-me-nots and sweet williams will still be in flower in early summer when it is almost time to think about sowing seed for flowering next year.

Remember to water your flowers regularly in dry weather; early summer is usually the driest time of the year.

Flowering shrubs

Trim off the dead-heads of winter-flowering heathers in early summer (the best way is to clip them off with shears). This keeps the plants compact and new shoots soon appear, to bear flowers during the winter and spring.

Prune early summer-flowering shrubs like *Olearia stellulata*, *Viburnum opulus* 'Roseum' and weigelas immediately after they have finished blooming. Cut out the old flowering branches, as this allows new ones to take their place. These will have flowers the following year.

Vegetables

Peas will be growing quickly and need pea sticks or special nets for support. Watch out for damage caused by tits and warblers as they sometimes will eat the young tender peas in their pods. Cover with nets if this happens.

Early summer is the right time for sowing runner beans, dwarf beans and sweet corn in open ground. Scatter some slug pellets where these seed are sown as the young pea or sweet corn seedlings are very susceptible to slug and snail damage.

Keep sowing successions of lettuce and radish seed to give a continuous supply throughout the summer months. Never sow too much seed; only sufficient for your needs.

If you have grown outdoor tomatoes from seed under glass, they can be planted outside in early summer when the risk of frosts have passed. Also plant out young courgette and marrow plants.

The watering of vegetables during summer is most important: you will never get tender well-grown vegetables if they are allowed to get too dry. Give them a really good watering about once a week rather than small amounts nearly every day, as this will only bring the roots to the surface which then get baked in hot weather.

● *Harvesting vegetables* Always harvest vegetables when they are young and tender and never let them get old and woody. This applies to peas, beans, carrots and beetroot (any surplus crops can be frozen). Cut lettuce when needed, although some are bound to run up to seed in hot weather.

In the middle of summer, shallots and onions need to be pulled up and laid out to dry, then they are stored in shallow boxes, hung in nets or strung up.

After peas and broad beans have been harvested, pull up the old plants and any pea sticks, and lightly rake over the soil. Then sow rows of turnips and swedes in their place. If you cannot eat them all by autumn they can be dug in as green manure.

Fruit

Summer is an extremely busy time in the garden especially of you grow lots of soft fruit.

The first thing to do is to weed around the fruit bushes before putting on nets to stop the birds eating the ripening fruit. This should be done in early summer as blackbirds will eat half-ripe strawberries and raspberries.

Early summer can be quite hot and dry, therefore give the soft fruit plenty of water to help produce large juicy fruits. A thick mulch helps to retain the moisture.

● *Harvesting fruit* Gooseberries are the first soft fruit to ripen, but you can pick them while they are still green, just leaving a few to ripen properly as they are delicious eaten raw. One of the best dessert varieties of gooseberry is 'Leveller' which produces very large juicy fruit.

Strawberries and raspberries should be picked every other day, otherwise they will go mouldy, especially in damp conditions. Excess crops can be made into delicious jam or jelly and can also be frozen.

Pick red and white currants when ready and use to make jelly or to mix with fresh fruit salads.

When picking blackcurrants you can prune the bush at the same time. Just cut out the branches with the fruit on them, then strip off the fruit.

When loganberries and blackberries have all been picked, the old fruiting wood can be cut out and the new canes tied in. If the new canes are not tied in during the summer they are likely to get damaged by winds.

Raspberries need to be treated in the same way, removing old canes. With raspberries, only keep the strong canes, snipping out very thin weedy ones.

● *Renewing strawberry plants* Do not keep strawberry plants longer than three years; after that they should be replaced. You can save some of your own runners or buy new stock. Work out how many replacement plants you need and just save that amount of runners. They will make strong plants more quickly if they are pegged down properly. Some people like to half-bury small pots filled with compost near the old strawberry plants and peg down a runner in each pot. When rooted, cut off from the main plant (this is usually in late summer). Then they will be ready to start a new row of strawberries. The earlier you plant new strawberries, the more fruit they will produce in their first year.

If your strawberries have very small fruit it is best to buy new virus-resistant plants.

● *Stone fruit* If you have old neglected plum, damson and cherry trees, prune them in summer, otherwise they are likely to get silver leaf (a fungus disease which causes branches and new shoots to die back). Always have a sharp pair of secateurs that cut cleanly without damaging the bark.

Plants in containers

Many people tend to grow more colourful plants in containers for summer interest than they do for winter and spring plantings.

Early summer is the best time to plant half-hardy annuals in pots, tubs and other interesting containers. Petunias, trailing lobelias, ageratum, alyssum and impatiens are all ideal for this use and will give you months of colour. Half-hardy perennials can also be used with great effect and these include marguerites, pelargoniums and heliotrope, which all look wonderful in clay pots or old stone urns and will flower non-stop all summer. Fuchsias are also excellent for any type of containers, as well as both fibrous-rooted and tuberous begonias.

▶ **Make good use of of any available wall space to provide a colourful background to perennial borders.**

Make sure that containers do not dry out completely in hot weather; they often need watering once a day.

Feed once a week with liquid fertilizer. It is best to use a special container and hanging basket fertilizer.

The plants must be dead-headed regularly for continuous flowering.

AUTUMN

Flowers

Autumn is the busiest time of the year for the amount of work to be done in the herbaceous border. The dead flower stems need to be cut down to ground level unless you are saving any ornamental seed heads or just saving seed to increase your stock. Cut off the old stems as near to the base as possible; if hollow stems are left they provide good hibernating places for slugs, snails and woodlice in dry weather. In wet weather they will fill up with water which sometimes will rot the crown of the plant.

Some perennials like Michaelmas daises and *Physostegia virginiana* 'Vivid' will still be flowering and should not be cut down yet.

Remove any dead or rotting leaves of the perennials, as again they provide shelter for slugs and snails during winter, appearing on mild days to eat the basal growth.

There are always some perennials which grow very vigorously during summer and need to be divided in autumn. Some varieties of hardy geraniums, hemerocallis and hostas will need to be split up about every three or four years. Dig up the plant and split the roots into about four pieces. This can be done by chopping up the plant with a spade, or using two forks back to back to lever the plant apart (Fig. 22). Replant just small

Fig. 22 Most perennials are very easy to divide and one clump can be split into two or more plants.

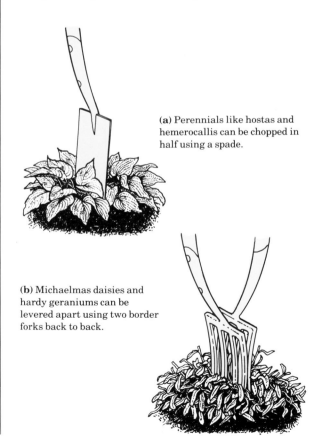

(a) Perennials like hostas and hemerocallis can be chopped in half using a spade.

(b) Michaelmas daisies and hardy geraniums can be levered apart using two border forks back to back.

pieces, forking bonemeal and well-rotted manure into the soil at the same time.

By now most hardy annuals will have finished blooming, so can be pulled up and put on your compost heap to rot down during the winter months. The same applies to half-hardy annuals.

Plant out biennials like wallflowers and forget-me-nots for spring-bedding displays; interplant with tulips and daffodils. Grow dwarf bulbs in front of these, such as *Anemone blanda*, chiono-doxias and crocuses.

Dig up dahlia tubers and gladioli corms and dry thoroughly before storing for the winter.

● *Taking cuttings* Early autumn is the time to take soft-wood cuttings of marguerites, pelar-goniums, half-hardy salvias and fuchsias. Put several cuttings round the edge of a pot, keep just damp and keep in a warm position until well rooted. Then pot up individually.

Leaf stem cuttings (Fig. 23), taken as flowers begin to fade, are a useful way of propagating perennials that are difficult to divide.

Shrubs

Unless the ground is very wet or frozen, new shrubs can be planted from late autumn onwards and existing shrubs moved if they are in the wrong place. Fork bonemeal or well-rotted manure into the soil before planting. Firm down the soil round the shrub really well to stop it rocking in windy weather. Some shrubs may need staking to stop this happening. Water the shrubs in dry weather until established.

Hardwood cuttings can be taken now of all kinds of shrubs, including evergreen ones like *Osmanthus delavayii* and the very attractive variegated box, which is wonderful when grown as a low hedge. Hardwood cuttings taken in the autumn will have rooted by spring.

Fig. 23 Leaf stem cuttings – a different way of propagating hesperis and moisture-loving lobelias.

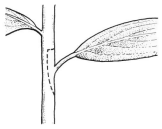

(a) Cut out a small section of stem with a leaf attached. This cutting should be about 2.5 cm (1 in) long and should be taken when the flowers on the top of the stem are beginning to die.

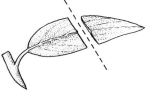

(b) As leaves are quite big, cut in half before putting the cutting into a suitable compost in a seed tray.

(c) Gently push cutting under the surface, making sure that the small piece of stem is in contact with the soil. Keep damp, but not too wet. They really need under-soil heat to root quickly. Pot up when clusters of tiny leaves appear in the leaf joint.

Vegetables

There is still plenty of different types of vegetables to be harvested. Sweet corn is ready for picking when the tassels turn dark brown in early autumn. Pick the last of the runner beans unless you are saving some for seed; these pods have to

91

◄ Michaelmas daisies are a 'must' for excellent early autumn colour in a cottage garden, also a good plant for attracting bees and butterflies.

► Vegetables and fruit, including potatoes and apples, stored ready for use during the winter months.

be left on until they look brown and dry. Store the seeds in a cool dry place ready for sowing the following year.

Cabbage, sprouts, leeks and parsnips will be ready for harvesting throughout the autumn.

Potatoes should be dug up the early autumn, dried and damaged ones put to one side before the rest are stored in a cool but frost-free place for the winter.

● *Storing root vegetables* Carrots, beetroot and parsnips can be lifted, the soil washed off them, then when dry, stored in dry sand or peat in boxes, or frozen if preferred.

Clean the ground where all the vegetables have been harvested, ready for digging over. Dig out a trench, putting the soil at the end of the vegetable plot where the digging finishes to fill in the empty trench. Dig in manure as required, or your own rotted compost can be used instead.

Fruit
Finish pruning any soft fruit that has not already been done. Weed between the plants before mulching the ground with a thick layer of well-rotted manure or spent mushroom compost.

Prunings of currants and gooseberries can be used for hardwood cuttings.

Pick apples and pears, store in tray for the winter in a cool, frost-free position. Check these fruit from time to time, taking out any that have rotted. Use damaged or partly rotted apples for making purée, which can be frozen most successfully.

Plants in containers
Remove all half-hardy annuals and perennials from your containers, ready for planting them up with winter and spring-flowering bulbs inter-planted with wallflowers, forget-me-nots, polyan-thus, primroses and the lovely flowering pansies.

Camellias, skimmias, winter and spring-flowering heathers and dwarf conifers are excellent for growing in containers to give interesting displays from flowers and foliage throughout the winter months.

Do not allow containers to get too dry. This is especially true when growing camellias as the buds will turn brown and fall off. In dry, frosty weather, only water containers in the middle of the day as you do not want the water to freeze on the plants.

In extremely cold conditions, move small containers to a sheltered position or wrap them up in sacking or plastic sheeting to stop frost from damaging their roots.

WINTER

Flowers

Finish cutting down your perennials, take out any remaining weeds and make any final planting changes.

Apply a thick mulch of spent mushroom compost or well-rotted manure between the perennials. This will feed them for the next flowering season.

To protect perennials that are likely to suffer from slug and snail damage, surround the plants with dry moss peat, forest bark or coarse grit. This works successfully with plants like hostas and delphiniums.

Flowering shrubs

Check that there is no further pruning needed and that all shrubs are in good shape. Rake up any dead leaves and pieces of twigs from under the shrubs and remove any weeds, especially any perennial ones. Cover bare soil with pulverized forest bark – a good mulch for under trees and shrubs, suppressing many weeds. Bare soil can also be covered by the use of ground-cover perennials; hardy geraniums, ajuga, hostas and lamiums are all good for this purpose.

With all this work done there is little or no maintenance during the rest of the winter months, apart from raking up any leaves and twigs.

Vegetables

Put nets over cabbages, Brussels sprouts and sprouting broccoli to stop the pigeons eating the leaves. Pigeons can be very destructive in the winter and will completely strip the plants of foliage in a few days unless prevented.

Finish off any digging and leave fallow. Unless your soil is chalky, spread lime over the ground in early winter, as it helps to sweeten the soil; then all that is needed is first to rake over the ground before planting begins again in the spring.

Other jobs for the winter

If the weather is suitable, try to make a late cut of your lawn as this should be done in early winter. It will cut off any tough pieces of grass and pick up leaves at the same time. A tidy lawn is the finishing touch to a well-kept garden. When the lawn has been cut for the last time, give your mower a good overhaul before putting it away for the winter.

Check and clean all tools and put them away neatly, ready for when you need them in the spring.

Clean and tie up in bunches canes and metal stakes to be put away for the winter.

If you can manage to complete all this work before the middle of winter you might be lucky to have a couple of free months before gardening starts in earnest again in early spring. This will give you time to work out planting plans and order seeds for the new season.

Index

Page numbers in *italics* indicate an illustration or boxed table.